THE FUTURE

OF

INSURANCE

From Disruption to Evolution

Volume I. The Incumbents

Lessons From Legacy Insurers
Succeeding In A Changing Industry

BRYAN FALCHUK

Insurance Evolution Press 📖

Published by Insurance Evolution Press
Boston, Massachusetts

DEDICATION

This book is dedicated to the hundreds of thousands of hard-working people of the Insurance industry who are there for others in their toughest moments, when their need is greatest, putting lives back together.

CONTENTS

FOREWORD from CARIBOU HONIG

One of the most over-used terms in the insurance and insurtech space is "disruption." After all, it is even part of the title of this book. I do not believe we are going to see much actual disruption, though. Instead, I believe what we will see – and are already seeing – is transformation or evolution. Let me explain the difference.

Disruption is when the whole industry structure gets flipped on its head. Think about what ride sharing has done to the taxi industry, what online travel sites did to the travel agent business, and what has happened to media over the last 20 years with the advent of digital and streaming media. The impact of insurtech on the industry may be profound but it will not be disruptive.

Instead, I see evolution, which is about change rather than a complete upending. Yes, there may be pieces or parts of the value chain that will see disruption. For example, particular kinds of claims adjusters may see their work automated or even 'outsourced to customers,' which would have real disruptive impact on those people and their role in the value chain. Advanced risk modeling with machine learning may disrupt actuaries, and the use of those models may disrupt underwriters as the intelligence of the tools reduces the need for quite so many human beings to evaluate and interpret risk. And there has been vast debate about whether certain agents or brokers will be disrupted by the rise of digital distribution channels, a debate that has stretched back to the early days of the Internet (though has still not proven out).

Despite the very real disruption pieces of the value chain may experience, for the most part, the industry structure is not getting disrupted at the macro level. Some new players will capture some of the profit pool from the players of today. There are opportunities for new segments of the population to be served in new ways, or the creation of entirely new products. With these open, greenfield possibilities, it is yet to be decided who will jump into these spaces, and who will win in them.

It is not always the insured who are being targeted by insurtech startups. Incumbent carriers are increasingly being served by many enabling, B2B insurtech solutions trying to help those incumbents serve their customers. While these enabling solutions may be the source of some localized disruption, their intention is not to unseat incumbents. They instead focus on helping incumbents operate more efficiently, and, more importantly, to be faster, nimbler, and more flexible in serving the insured. In this way, these enabling insurtech solutions also help guard incumbents against the startup carriers trying to 'drink incumbents' milkshake'.

These startup carriers come to market with a much cleaner slate than incumbents. *De novo* carriers are free from the constraints of legacy tech stack, legacy processes, legacy channels, legacy underwriting models and so on. They are able to more-freely pick and choose how they assemble their value chain. Incumbents can use the help of enabling insurtechs to offset this advantage. The whole dynamic can be viewed as a race to see whether incumbents will effectively leverage B2B insurtech solutions before the startups, unshackled from legacy constraints, crack the code on unit economics and scalability.

This builds an 'us vs. them' mentality, as if to imply there can be only one winner – the incumbents or the startups. This is a false dichotomy.

Realistically, major incumbent carriers do not really need to worry about startups like Lemonade, Root, Hippo, Next, Vault or others. They should pay attention to these new carriers and learn from them, but they need not wake up sweating in the middle of the night at the idea of being put out of business by the startups.

The bigger threat to incumbents likely comes from tech titans and the most successful FinTech players expanding into insurance. For example, a greater threat to an auto insurer likely comes from car companies, tech giants like Amazon and Tencent or FinTechs like Credit Karma. That threat compounds in the event that these non-insurance companies combine their vast resources with an insurtech carrier. An incumbent could likely fend off a startup carrier or a tech powerhouse on their own, but fending off their combined forces is far more daunting.

If this represents the real threat you might face as an incumbent, what should your strategy be? To what extent do you prioritize refactoring your legacy tech stack by aggressively leveraging what insurtechs have built? Or do you adopt the philosophy, "If you can't beat them, join them," and partner with one of these potential new competitors, enabling their solution? Or do you simply demur: you might look at your legacy business and see it as just that, a legacy. You can incrementally invest in it, and decide that full-bore embracing of insurtech is simply not worth it.

With the starting point of operating an existing insurance business, the opportunity may be to take what you have and use it to enable the customer-facing insurtechs. They are building next generation products for segments that may have newly-arisen (like gig economy workers), been ignored, overlooked, or underserved. Enabling their success may prove to be a better decision than competing head-to-head, particularly given the investment required to refactor your own technology stack to catch up to their legacy-free starting point.

You could also choose to leave your legacy business as-is, while simultaneously building a new business unit to compete in the greenfield spaces revealed by the startups. This is a viable path, as well, but recognize that it is a *different* path. Each of these strategies will require focus and investment that becomes hard to sustain simultaneously.

In many ways the strategy question boils down whether you choose to play offense or defense, and to what extent. Do you play offense and leverage insurtech to grow the top-line? Or do you play defense and deploy technology to refactor your own capabilities with an emphasis on efficiency, speed, and agility?

No matter which path you choose, there are real tradeoffs to be made. This is not just about investments or technology decisions, but the creation of a cascade of related choices. For example, consider distribution partnerships. Would you focus on trying to partner with a tech giant (for example, Tencent) or with a financial services giant (for example, Citibank); would you partner with an incumbent channel partner (for example, Marsh or Brown & Brown) or an outsider or startup (for example, ADP or Bunker).

With all these decisions, there are traps for both incumbents and startups. Many insurance executives spend too much time worrying about the change management associated with the technology aspect, or overweight the extent to which their legacy technology is holding them back. And entrepreneurs may be giving too much credence to the notion that they are free from legacy constraints and therefore have an inevitable path to success.

In reality, there is an argument to be made that legacy *culture* more than technology is what truly holds back the incumbents. That is echoed directly by the case studies in this book as none of the takeaway insights from these cases are actually about technology. At the same time, we see that the entrepreneurial mindset is more at play in the success of startups than their freedom from legacy technology and processes. In this distinction of culture between incumbents and startups is the biggest opportunity for the evolution of the industry.

While the differing mindsets of many incumbents and startups may make it challenging to come together, this is also where the greatest opportunity lies. When you can collaborate to extract the best of both cultures so you can be nimble *yet* resilient, good at risk taking *and* risk management, that is where the magic happens in creating the future of insurance.

– Caribou Honig
Chairman and Co-Founder, InsureTech Connect

PREFACE

This book was being written as the global COVID-19 pandemic was in its infancy, and the text was being finalized as the US started to see most states telling people to stay home. While the pandemic is not the theme of this book, I felt compelled to say something about it as this is a very difficult and strange time for everyone on this planet, to say the least.

This book does not address the pandemic or its impact as the cases shared here pre-date the emergence of it. That is not to say it has no impact on the people or companies in the cases in this book, their customers and partners, or the world at large. Indeed, it does. It is also not to imply that the condition we all find ourselves in as the severity of the situation increased is irrelevant to the topic of being able to innovate. Of course, it does.

At the same time, we should not assume that COVID-19 or its impact on our lives means evolution is impossible or needs to stop in its entirety. Indeed, many companies had to evolve in an instant, suddenly virtualizing their staff through remote working, halting travel, and finding new solutions to delivering claims service when existing solutions were impacted or no longer available.

If there is anything this industry has proven throughout its history is its resilience. We are there for people in their toughest moments to help them piece their lives back together. You cannot do that if you are not resilient yourself because it is hard work that takes an emotional toll, and you would quickly be unable to go on without this essential strength. We are an industry of people who face challenges, who see extreme devastation, and we do not pause or cower. We step up and help. We find solutions.

This is no doubt difficult, and the people of the industry are not just watching a catastrophe they will help deal with, but are living it themselves, making it even harder. Yet with new types of tools and solutions available, and the need for them increased in many ways by the current situation, now is exactly the time to think about our evolution.

This is a moment we will look back on and ask people, "What did you do with the time?" Did you sit back and wait for it to be over? Did you leave room for others who were not content to pause, but rather used this as a chance to rethink their business beyond just allowing people to work from home? Or did you decide to evolve what you do and how you do it to ensure your relevance and strength in the future of insurance?

I. PRE-HISTORY

Before we begin, I wanted to share how we got here, or more accurately, how *I* got here. By understanding my story, you will understand how this book came to be, and should have a deeper appreciation for why I felt it *had* to be in the first place.

In the Spring of 2000 as I finished college, I accepted a job with Boston-based Liberty Mutual in their internal strategy consulting team. I wanted to be a management consultant coming out of college, and this seemed like a great opportunity to do consulting work at a time when my classmates were having job offers rescinded (if they got one at all) because the economy was melting down in the Dot Com Bubble Burst of 1999.

I did not intend to work in insurance (this is something I often hear veterans of the industry say as part of telling their insurance career story), but in my first interaction with the industry, I saw its legendary stability first-hand. While many employers were pulling back, insurance was still hiring, so I had a job to go to after graduation.

Since my days in Corporate Strategy & Research, as the consulting team is now called, I went on to work in Liberty's US Personal Lines business (which did not include the regional and national carriers they bought, like Safeco, Indiana Insurance, Ohio Casualty, Peerless and others). I got to work on a wide range of issues, including several customer experience and technology projects, giving me a taste for how those two themes can play together for mutual benefit or by one, technology, standing in the way of the other, customer experience, as was historically the case in our industry.

I left Liberty to pursue my MBA at Dartmouth College's Tuck School of Business. In my internship during business school and full-time after school, I worked in the insurance practice of McKinsey &

Company doing some really interesting and impactful work in the US and Europe on Commercial and Personal lines, including getting my first exposure to Specialty Lines. I worked on growth, distribution, M&A, post-merger integration and Claims projects, setting the stage for my return to working for a carrier again.

I left McKinsey to join British Specialist Beazley, as they grew their fledgling US business. That was an incredibly exciting time as we grew from a very small business into what is today a more-than $1 billion operation. Globally, the entire company I joined at the start of 2008 was smaller than the US team alone is today. I got to work in an underwriting team, built out the distribution function, and eventually I was responsible for Underwriting and Claims Operations across the US. I was also the lead business representative on a new core system we were building in-house, and was deeply involved in the day-to-day of this incredibly complex, expensive project first-hand. We also had early desires from brokers to get quotes electronically, as the industry was by-now doing regularly in Personal Lines and core Commercial products like Auto. And we struggled, using duct tape and glue (or Excel and people, more accurately) so as not to lose the opportunities we were seeing despite our technology not being up to the task.

After Beazley, I briefly worked at a Medical Malpractice carrier, seeing a microcosm of the industry that faces many different constraints and challenges the rest of P&C does not face, including a disappearing customer-base as medical providers were merging into larger, often self-insured entities. This created a true existential crisis for Med Mal carriers who had decades of investments in their platform as insurance companies and not simply to serve as TPAs, which was increasingly what was being demanded by larger and larger healthcare providers. The sentiment, "Evolve or Die", was a growing war cry within the space.

In leaving the Med Mal carrier, I got my first taste of the innovative world of Tech when I joined safety-technology startup Guardhat, to build out their partnerships with Workers' Compensation insurers and help secure venture capital (VC) funding. While Guardhat is a successful business today with offices and employees, I joined while it was still an idea the founders worked on in one of their garages. It was incredibly exciting helping to create something from the ground up, and seeing how the data from their smart hardhat and safety equipment could empower a potential revolution in Workers' Compensation insurance.

The biggest problem I see in Workers' Compensation is the asymmetry of information. Carriers do not *really* know what the exposure is since they cannot see the true risk employees face day-to-day. They send risk engineers on site to observe things, and employees all follow the safety rules when representatives from the carrier or safety inspectors are on site for observation. However, you never know what these same employees do when the carrier's representatives aren't there. Safety equipment, such as hard hats, may not be worn, areas with restricted access may be freely walked through as short-cuts and warning, signs, lights and alert tones may be ignored. Or carriers may presume as much and bake into their rating an assumed-non-compliance rate for these safety measures even if they are being followed.

This means carriers are rating the policy somewhat blindly, potentially giving discounts that should not be given, or perhaps over-charging for risk that is not there. And for insureds, it feels like they're always over-paying for insurance *and* lost-time, especially in the high-risk, heavy industrial space on which Guardhat focuses. As a result, it's no wonder profitability has always been difficult in Workers' Comp, and Guardhat had a way to change that while saving lives.

While at Guardhat, I was presented the opportunity to join another British Specialist's US business when Hiscox USA was looking for a new Head of Claims. I spent the next three years working with the most amazing people at a carrier who had done something extremely bold, go direct in Commercial and Specialty Lines while also building a broker-sold business. In the three years I was at Hiscox, the business doubled, creating all kinds of stresses, but the team went after it every day with an energy and purpose I've not seen many other places, and that made it incredibly fun and exciting.

While at Hiscox, I also was introduced to an insurtech startup called Hi Marley, which was looking to fix the communication problems that were brewing as people increasingly do not answer their phones, emails and voicemails go days without a response, and consumer expectations to be able to communicate digitally with the businesses they work with increases. Hi Marley enables carriers to text with insureds in a compliant, flexible way. In my infinite wisdom, I did not see the point. Luckily, my team did, and we decided to do a pilot of their solution, and quickly signed on as one of their first full customers.

That set the stage for me to grow a relationship with the founders, becoming an advisor to the company. Eventually, this resulted in me joining the team to help grow the business, which I'm excited to look at today as more than just a bet, but a thriving provider of a truly-impactful solution many great carriers are using, including one in this book.

It was in my capacity as Head of Growth for Hi Marley that I met with countless carriers who really seemed to be struggling with the vise-like pressure of disruptive threats on one side and a sense of being unable to innovate on the other. In helping several carriers pilot and implement Hi Marley as I had done at Hiscox, I felt a pressing need to tell the story of carriers, who have been able to rise above the constraints they face to find ways to evolve how they deliver insurance products and services to their insureds.

This is how the idea for *The Future of Insurance: from Disruption to Evolution* was born. Along my journey, I had built a relationship with the Insurance Nerds, who I shared the idea with, and worked together to bring this project to reality.

This book is broken into three sections, with the first providing background on the situation we find ourselves in today as an industry. The second moves into case studies of seven carriers who have done something innovative and creative to evolve that sheds light on key success factors to consider in your business. Finally, the last section brings these lessons together to give a cohesive idea of how an industry that faces many headwinds and handcuffs can evolve how it thinks about and delivers on its promise to standby people at their most difficult moments regardless of the disruptive threats that may crop up today or in the future.

You should feel free to read it cover-to-cover if you want the full story, including the framing background of the current situation, all of the various ways different carriers have done something to evolve, and how to bring it all together in the end.

You may also find value in reading (or even going back and re-reading) specific cases of carriers who did something in a space you are working on, or perhaps a case that especially resonates with you because that specific insurer faces similar dynamics to what you face in your business. Each case is self-contained and can stand alone, though the greatest value lies in the combined power of the learning that comes from the sum of what they all discovered through their journeys. None of the cases is meant to be a blueprint for implementing one specific solution in the exact way that particular insurer did. Instead, they are meant to give guidance, inspiration, challenge and ideas for you consider as you look at evolving your business as the environment shifts around us.

While this book obviously focuses purely on the insurance industry, the lessons in it extend well beyond that. Whether you work at a carrier, insurtech provider, insurance ecosystem partner like a broker or agent or are in a different industry entirely, this book contains valuable insights about innovation that should extend to your context.

With that background, let's look at a disruptive period the industry faced at the turn of the twenty-first century, which sets the stage for the new disruptive period we are in the midst of as we cross into the 2020s.

1. The First Disruption

I got so much out of my initial experience at Liberty Mutual, a company that was about one-third the size of the present-day incarnation of itself when I joined. I got exposure across Personal and Commercial lines, both domestically and abroad, and worked on projects spanning all major functions – distribution (both direct and intermediated), service, technology, M&A, corporate structure, product, etc. I also got exposure to this new(ish) thing called "The Internet" that was threatening how we had always done business. To give you a sense of how early it was in the Internet's life, Google was still a small player in search, with most of its larger competitors at the time being companies that do not exist today.

The new idea was that people might actually want to get an insurance quote online, if not buy and service their policy there, too. Brokers and agents, it was foretold, would cease to exist as online aggregators and portals with names starting with "E" (the prefix "i" had not yet been invented by Apple, apparently) or ending with "Exchange" (or some clever misspelling of the word) cropped up left and right.

What we were looking at was disruption in a major way. While it was never clear which disruptive threats would materialize and actually cause a shift, it always felt clear that we would not be able to keep up with it and, therefore, faced a high probability of being left behind. And if we were not left behind, our broker and agent partners or Liberty's investment in its direct sales force and local office network would be.

This was a scary time.

The fear was not irrational. We faced many good reasons to believe we would be left out in the cold, and we were not alone in these thoughts.

Insurance is heavily regulated, so managing this sort of disruption across regulators in fifty states plus those in various international jurisdictions was complicated, if not a complete non-starter. Having to file product changes, wait for approval, get licenses, risk running afoul of existing regulations with our actions, etc., are all serious issues.

And if our compliance constraints could be mitigated, how would we navigate channel conflict effectively? Would our brokers stop sending us business if we participated in one of these online exchanges? Would our sales staff quit and try to move their customers to a competitor if we started quoting online? What about our technology? Could we even make all of this work when we've struggled to meet timelines, budgets or scope with technology projects before?

"Many of the recent insurtech startups will fail....it is highly likely that the vast majority of them will go bankrupt if history is any guide. But it would be foolish to bet that all of them will."

– Rob Galbraith from "The End of Insurance As We Know It"

You know how the story played out. Despite those fears and the disruptive threats around, not only did Liberty Mutual survive and thrive, but so did most carriers (and those who did not were not taken down by E-commerce disruption). Agent and broker channels were also able to survive. Despite all the threat and doomsday predictions, the industry players and dynamics remained largely unchanged, but with some new tools growing up around us.

Why is that? How was it that the industry that has stood by people in their moments of greatest need and supported people in pursuing their dreams without risk standing in their way survived despite all of this fear and these constraints?

Rather than dig into the insights from the early 2000s, this book looks into another, similar time, which we are living in right now, the age of the insurtech disruptor. The disruptive threat is so strong, it spawned a book by industry veteran Rob Galbraith, ominously entitled *The End of Insurance As We Know It*. While Galbraith does not actually foretell the end of insurance in its entirety, he talks in great detail about the disruptive threats and enabling solutions carriers can use to counter those threats.

While it may be tempting to swear off these new threats, Galbraith gives a balanced interpretation to what we should expect of these startup carriers. He writes that "many of the recent insuretech startups and similar ventures will fail. In fact, it is highly likely that the vast majority of them will go bankrupt if history is any guide. But it would be foolish to bet that *all of them* will fail, and there is a fair likelihood that one or more will succeed wildly in the way that Uber has in the ride-sharing industry and Airbnb has in the home-sharing space." [Emphasis added][1]

Andy Stevenson, who was responsible for global Claims operations and running European Claims for Hiscox while I was there, summed up the history and set the context we face currently when he said:

> "The insurance industry has certainly evolved; door-to-door salespeople with paper folders to online full-lifecycle management on a smart phone is a large step. In the context of a 100-plus-year time-line, this may not feel as big a change as offered by the 'innovators' and 'disruptors' of today, where digital technology allows a more rapid progression; but this needs to be put back into context."

The argument today is not just about disrupting pieces of the insurance equation, but rather entire carriers. Or, perhaps more accurately, the way consumers define the meaning of insurance as a product they buy.

Full-stack, startup carriers are promising to deliver insurance products and services in a modern, flexible, digital way that gives you only what you need without charging you for what you don't, and not bogging you down in how you get service when you need it. And because there's no legacy baggage, they may be able to do it smarter, faster, cheaper and better.

Without naming names, several startup carriers have made huge splashes, and done a fantastic job marketing their brand on the back of the idea that insurance is broken, and that being a customer of the slate of incumbent insurers is miserable. They have focused on

---

[1] Galbraith, Robert, *The End of Insurance As We Know It*, Insurance Nerds, 2019, pg. 9.

delivering materially better customer experiences using a new generation of tools, free from legacy system-constraints, resistance to change (or even having a historical way of working to have to resist changing from), bureaucracy or memories of past failed projects. They also do not have decades of regulatory complications holding them back. In short, they are admirable adversaries posing a real threat.

Yet, despite that threat, and despite some excellent customer experience (or "CX") successes, they have also struggled.

Their underwriting results leave much to be desired, though that's true for most startup or small carriers as they build their book of business to a large-enough scale to smooth results. Early, poor combined ratio performance is not enough to dismiss a startup as a flash in the pan. Yet, at the same time, their performance may be poor for reasons beyond an inability to smooth losses, such as inexperience handling claims effectively; not having rich, historical data to inform product, rating and claims decisions; hubris around being smarter than the insurance industry causing you to miss the nuances that the industry has learned really do matter, etc.

Essentially, it is too early for most of these startups to know if they could be viable as insurers or not, and certainly too early to claim victory.

Their struggle has been on the delivery of the core of what it means to be an insurer; transferring and managing risk while effectively managing the capital associated with that risk transfer.

If you look into customer reviews of many of the startup carriers, once you get past the fantastic buying experience, you tend to see a different story.

One person I interviewed, who was shopping for condo insurance, and had been leaning toward a startup due to price and simplicity, was angry after seeing customer ratings and reviews from people who had claims or tried to make changes on their policy. She used the word "horrible" when describing what it was like to be insured by them if you ever needed to make a claim. While it was easy to *become* insured by them, it was painful to *be* insured by them, according to her research. Incumbent carriers have been doing that crucial part of the equation much better for well over a century.

Yet, despite being able to manage capital and risk, there is much to be desired in how we, as an industry, have kept up with changing customer expectations. And as startup carriers push the envelope on the CX front, expectations become demands. This is where the mandate to evolve comes from, our customers' evolving expectations. Whether these startups succeed or not is not the issue. Some will, some won't, just like the players in the search engine space when Google was starting up. What matters is what they achieve in the time they have in terms defining a new set of expectations of what the insurance customer experience needs to be.

We are back in the same dilemma as the one the industry faced at the turn of the century; we need to evolve in the face of disruptors who are moving past us in terms of *how* we deliver insurance to the market.

But how can we? We face so many headwinds working against us. We are a highly-regulated industry.

We have disparate technology solutions that cost us huge sums of money and time to deploy (if they even get deployed fully). And these solutions cannot easily be adapted, even if IT had the resources available to do so, which they don't.

We have well-established distribution channels that would turn their backs on us if we do anything even remotely disintermediating to them.

We have bureaucracies that will take years to make a decision on any form of innovation, and we don't have a good way to know if we have made the right decision because of how long the tail can take to play out on these decisions.

We have hundreds or even thousands of people whose jobs would be in jeopardy if we started doing things differently. And we fear many of these people aren't comfortable with technology, so the training and change management burden is too big for us to deal with.

We cannot directly talk to our insureds to know what they really want since the agents and brokers we work with are protective of *their* relationships with *their* customers.

We have CAT season to worry about, so we can't do anything disruptive to our ability to serve our customers in those critical moments.

We don't have the budget for any of this, especially not with how much we've already spent on technology that isn't really delivering what we expected it to.

While I'm being purposely provocative and dramatic here, the list of headwinds is long and very real. And for many carriers, there are many more headwinds specific to their situation, and those additional concerns are also very real.

Yet, despite all these headwinds, several carriers *are* doing it, including the seven in this book, CSAA, CNA, SCIF, Ohio Mutual, EMPLOYERS, AXA XL and USAA.

And they aren't doing it simply because they are free of these headwinds, but *in spite* of their constraints. They have found ways to work through them rather than stop because of them. In those success stories lies the insights we can all benefit from to evolve in our situation.

The reality is that the days of massive technology projects that risk taking down the company to effect a small customer-facing change are either gone or going away. A new generation of solutions and tools has emerged allowing for flexible design, testing, deployment and adjusting as we learn and grow. The cost structure of these new solutions allows us to use what we need to when we need to, rather than committing huge sums and hoping we see a return. In short, our ability to evolve has been disrupted in our favor.

Going forward, you will see a series of case studies of carriers who have evolved how they operate in specific parts of their business. None of these case studies is meant to be carbon-copied into your business. Instead, the lessons contained within the case studies about how they went about implementing change is what you can take forward. You will see themes around people, culture, structure and more that each carrier used to break free of their particular set of headwinds to move the way they deliver insurance products and services to their customers forward.

This book is meant for people in the industry as a source of guidance, inspiration and understanding about how to evolve the delivery of insurance products and services. It is also meant more broadly to inspire us all to keep pushing the envelope to do better for our customers regardless of the constraints and threats we face.

It may be helpful to a manager, director, AVP, VP, etc., hoping to make change in your organization but unsure how to get past the barriers you face. Likewise, members of the C-Suite or Board of a carrier who is concerned about disruptive threats and sense of being stuck in addressing them can find the stories and discussion in this book useful in building a strategy for effective change to evolve your business. Or the various insurtech companies hoping to enable that evolution may find guidance on how to better understand your carrier-customers and help them ensure working with you is successful for you, them, their insureds and the rest of their partners in the insurance ecosystem.

Lastly, the disruptive startup carriers I mentioned above may also find value in this book to better-understand carriers you may be quick to underestimate in an industry you may think to be devoid of some of the complications that truly do exist in it. This may save you from making some missteps in your own journey, or may open you to thoughts of partnering with existing carriers, as some have done, rather than seeing them as competitors unable to keep up with you no matter how hard they try.

2. A Present Danger

Today's disrupting forces are slightly different than those from the past in that they are now being aimed directly at carriers in addition to other parts of the insurance ecosystem. Lemonade, Vouch, Root and others are building carriers from the ground up (so-called "full-stack" carriers) to directly take on the incumbents. Some are going at it from a hybrid model, starting as MGAs with carrier-backing, like Slice, Hippo and Trov. And others are morphing through various models, as Next has done, starting with an aim to disrupt agents, then becoming an MGA, now transforming into a carrier who is also looking to empower agents.

While there are still plenty of threats to other players in the value chain (for example, Honk for roadside assistance, Snapsheet for appraising and claims management, WeGoLook for field adjusting and evidencing), carriers themselves were not being targeted in the same way they are today.

What isn't clear, though, is whether these new entrants have legs or not. Based on the number of times they're mentioned in keynotes and panel discussions, Lemonade seems to be at every conference in the industry, though they rarely attend any events themselves. The buzz around these players is huge, even if their market share or financial success isn't (though their valuations may be, as evidenced by Next obtaining Unicorn status in October 2019 while Lemonade was valued at over $2 billion in their Spring 2019 funding round).

What is it that's so different about these players that creates a threat to incumbents? Or, more precisely, what gap in the offering today are they exploiting to create value, and are they uniquely qualified to capture that value in a way incumbent carriers are not and cannot be?

The answer to the second question, I believe, is a resounding, no. The answer to the first question can be found in how Lemonade founder Dan Shreiber describers the company. He said, "We are looking to create a dominant and technologically-enabled insurance company on a global basis."[2]

If we ignore the bombastic part about global domination, we see the focus is on enablement of the insurance product experience. There is nothing in that idea that cannot be applied to incumbent carriers. That is, being able to deploy technology creatively and in a way that empowers and delights consumers is not the sole domain of startup carriers, nor is there some insurmountable hurdle that only clean-sheet approaches can overcome.

> "The industry has outsourced the front end to agents, and so they did not directly see the development of the problem."
>
> – Jeff Goldberg
> EVP of Research & Consulting, Novarica

The dilemma we are left with is *why* the gap these startups are taking advantage of exists in the first place.

To dig into this question, I spoke to Jeff Goldberg of Novarica, a leading advisor to the industry on technology decisions and strategy. He shared an incredibly insightful comment on the situation. "The industry has outsourced the front end to agents, and so they did not directly see the development of the problem."

For most carriers, the front end of the customer experience, sales, service and even some of the upfront interaction during a claim, is outsourced to distribution partners such as brokers or agents. That means carriers are not getting that real-time, "at the coal face" feedback that is so crucial to know how and where to invest in CX. Unless they made a concerted effort to study changes in customer expectations, they had no natural mechanism to see what was happening and respond to it.

You could say that this doesn't hold up for the chunk of the market that is sold directly to consumers by carriers like GEICO, Progressive, Amica, USAA and others. What we find is that these direct players are generally lauded for the ease of doing business with them, which would seem to reinforce the value of learning first-hand what matters to consumers. Of course, it was the direct writers who were quoting and

---

[2] Stroller, Kristin, "Fintech Insurer Lemonade Valued At More Than $2 Billion After $300 Million Funding Deal," Forbes, April 11, 2019.

binding business online first, among other things. They were able to push the envelope given their more front-row-seat-to-the-party status.

Then you may ask why they were not able to close the gap the rest of the way? I think there are two main reasons.

First, I don't think many of us in the industry fully see the scale of the gap until it is shown to us by disruptors working to close it. This is actually very common across many industries. The most blatant is what Apple did with smartphones. And while you can think that didn't work out for the incumbents (it didn't for Nokia and Motorola, the two biggest at the time, or BlackBerry, the biggest smartphone maker at the time), it did work out well for another major player, Samsung, who quickly followed Apple's lead right to the top of the phone sales league table.

> "It may require some changes or decisions to change that are not trivial...But the bigger obstacle in practice is the legacy culture. But it's a choice."
>
> – Caribou Honig
> Co-Founder, InsureTech Connect

In the automotive world, once Tesla pushed hard enough, you started to see every major auto maker invest in EVs, with GM, Ford, Volkswagen and others pouring literally billions into their electric futures (as GM puts it). Once a few online stock brokers such as E*Trade and Ameritrade saw success in the late 1990s and early 2000s, the existing players pushed hard into the space and, today, firms like Schwab (who just bought TDAmeritrade) and Fidelity dominate. Disruptors showed the gap to incumbents, and those who woke up to the gap and closed it are still around.

The second reason incumbent carriers have struggled to close the gap, even when they are directly connected to customers, is where the headwinds discussed above come into play. This is where startups had an opportunity to think more freely and act more nimbly because they did not have any of the legacy costs that existing carriers did.

And that's ok.

The startup carriers took advantage of that freedom, and are pushing the envelope. The good news is that incumbent carriers can see what startups are doing, learn from it, and invest in their own evolution once they understand consumers demands.

Sometimes this is exactly what existing players need. As in many other industries that see disruptive new entrants, incumbents can become complacent, and stop pushing as hard as they could, or should, without a disruptive force from the outside stepping in. That disruption can come from a number of fronts, whether regulatory, economic, or from new competitors, as has been the case in insurance.

The question is whether it's too little, too late, or if incumbents really can evolve and thrive? Are the headwinds too strong, the legacy constraints too engrained, and disruptors too advantaged?

Galbraith put this question forward at the end of his book when he asks "whether or not these impacts remain on the fringes of the insurance ecosystem, where they are today, or whether they will move front and center in the insurance ecosystem tomorrow?"[3]

I discussed this question with Caribou Honig, co-founder of the largest insurtech conference in the world, InsureTech Connect (or ITC). He brought the matter together brilliantly. "The opportunity to close the innovation gap is available to insurers. It may not be easy, it may require some changes or decisions to change that are not trivial. Yes, there are aspects of the legacy tech stack that need to change and require investment. But the bigger obstacle in practice is the legacy culture. But it's a choice."

---

[3] Galbraith, pgs. 337-338.

3. The Rise of Incumbents

Despite the strength of the disruptive threat posed by startup, full-stack carriers, I do not ultimately see the end of the insurers as we've known them. As I said earlier, the new crop of disruptive carriers has done an excellent job of innovating on the CX side to meet the demands of a changed customer base. They have also done an exceptional job on their marketing message, punching well-above their weight.

At the same time, incumbent carriers have largely been involved in toe-to-toe price-driven marketing, promising bigger discounts, lower prices, more savings or other ways of saying the same thing, "we're cheaper." While we in the industry were busy focusing on price, which included a lot of innovation on our pricing models and cost-reducing claim handling-tools to support these lower rates, we focused less on the customer experience.

That balance in what we focus on can shift, and I'm seeing several incumbent carriers make a shift. Aiding this move, new insurtech solutions pop up seemingly-daily to help support a shift in the balance toward focusing more on the customer experience. The time has come for incumbent carriers to close the gap.

This gap exists in what I'd generally call the easy part of the insurance equation; delivering insurance products and services. That is not to say it is actually easy to do or do well, but it certainly is easy relative to effectively managing frequency, severity and the prediction of how the two will play out relative to your predictive rating on top of effective capital management at mega-scale, which is *really* hard.

These tough things are what I was referring to in Chapter 1 as what the startup carriers have struggled with while doing well on the CX front. And this is what (most) incumbents have (mostly) done well with through the undulations of the cycle. This is why I believe incumbents will ultimately be still successful in the long run.

Now, to be fair, I spent my career at, or consulting for, incumbents, so you may think I'm biased. I may be, and am not blind to my less-than-impartial vantage point. But that does not mean I'm wrong.

Looking at analogous industries, we have seen similar situations that ultimately play out in the incumbents' favor. That does not mean startups all fail or don't claim a meaningful place in the market. They very well can, and often do. But it also does not mean the old guard inherently must die off for the disruptors to succeed. As Caribou Honig put it when we spoke, "Relatively few people, whether incumbent or startup, would generally argue that insurance is a winner-take-all category." Few industries ever are.

Looking at telecom, we see an industry with many similarities to insurance: high levels of regulation, high levels of capital-intensity, historically-high barriers to entry that were almost instantaneously removed with the birth of the Internet (or IP telephony, specifically), and a business model that depends on large numbers of subscribers to smooth out the highs and lows of operating in such an environment.

In 2001, Vonage was started as an Internet-based alternative to traditional telecom providers like AT&T and Verizon. They marketed heavily as being a friendly, flexible alternative to traditional phone companies that offered services you actually wished you could get in a manner you wished you could get them. No more being stuck with offerings you didn't really want or value, sold in traditional, slow ways. They got a lot of attention, and there was a lot of talk about disruption.

With about 2.5 million customers today, you cannot say that Vonage failed. However, this pales in comparison to even the smallest traditional telecom companies they sought to disrupt. In just their wireless business, Verizon has over sixty-times as many customers.

Vonage got a lot of things right: flexible products more closely tied to what people truly wanted and needed, better value since you were only paying for what you needed and also not simultaneously paying for the huge capital investment in the copper and fiber telecom network Verizon and others built out and maintained, etc. That is, they did a great job at CX-type things. But Vonage also got a lot of the basics of being a telecom wrong. Their service delivery was spotty, with loads of complaints from customers on various review websites and even having to pay a penalty to thirty-two states in 2009 for services not meeting what they had advertised. That is, they struggled with the hard part of being a telecom service provider despite their hubris as a disruptor.

What Vonage and the VoIP disruptor movement did was wake the existing telecom hegemony up on a number of fronts. Service offerings have evolved with more digital capabilities, convergence or unification of services across devices, Software-as-a-Service (SaaS) options, and more competitive pricing and compelling value stories for consumers.

We are witnessing another example in the auto industry, where Telsa, Fisker Automotive, Faraday Future and other startup car makers sought to seize on the EV future while incumbent automakers remained stuck with internal combustion engines and compliance cars for the so-called "ZEV (zero-emissions vehicle) states" (California, and those following their emissions regulations, like my home state of Massachusetts).

Fisker and Faraday died fairly rapid deaths, with Fisker at least bringing its car, the Karma, to market (which is now reborn as Karma Automotive's Revero). Faraday is sort of still around though their funding dried up, and we shall see if their cars ever come to market. Tesla, as we all know, has been a success on many fronts, especially in the stock market where their valuation tops most traditional auto makers, and they are also finally profitable in their core business. Other startups show promise, like Rivian, who took a $500 million investment from Ford recently.

What you notice, though, is that the auto industry is still largely made up of the same players with similar shares of the market. If anything, Chinese auto makers like SAIC, Geely (who bought Volvo from Ford) and BAIC have eaten into more of the global market pie than Tesla or other disruptors.

Tesla has been able to thrive (and we can of course debate the definition of the word "thrive" here), while incumbents have been able to coexist.

Tesla has pushed the auto industry in many meaningful ways, from the most obvious push of building truly competitive EVs, to perhaps less obvious areas like over-the-air updates of your car's software and features. It's also hard to imagine that car makers would be experimenting with subscription models and other alternative purchasing approaches if not for Tesla's direct sales through their own stores (not dealerships) and the web. To be sure, whether Tesla is a success or not depends on how you define the term, the industry has been impacted positively by the push it has given, and we are unlikely to see a world where most of the current top car makers fade into obscurity as a result of Tesla's disruptive push. That may be a fate that befalls some of them still, but it is unlikely that Tesla will be the reason for it.

> "The people who were really innovating at the time aren't here anymore. They ran out of cash or got acquired, but forced the incumbents to get their stuff together."
>
> – Kevin Kerridge
> EVP, Hiscox USA

In exploring the question of whether incumbents can win, I spoke with my former colleague, Kevin Kerridge, who setup Hiscox's direct business in the UK and the US.

Kerridge is a bit unique in that he is a disruptor in many ways, though also very much part of an incumbent carrier. That perspective gives him insight into this question that I find extremely valuable. Like me, he sees opportunity and possibility for incumbents. Kerridge talked specifically about a shift in how we can seize on this opportunity in noting the recent changes to the tools we have at our disposal to evolve, like cloud and SaaS solutions or the growth of APIs to connect disparate systems and tools in ways that would have taken massive integration efforts in the past. An API, which stands for Application Programming Interface, is basically a set of tools, processes and instructions that allow one system or service to interact with another. For example, if you log into a website using your Google or Facebook login information, that website is using Google or Facebook's APIs to tap into their secure login tools.

These are all incremental tools, but in aggregate, they enable a true evolution from where we have been. They just do so in a simpler way than legacy tools could have done before. That is a pivotal shift for us.

Andy Stevenson added clarity to this idea, as well:

> "Likely more successful strategies will be to find answers that require less commitment; where adoption can be trialed, assessed and then easily swapped out in the future – a move away from one enormous engine doing everything, to an ordered collection of services that can be traded, swapped, and upgraded without needing wholesale change."

Kerridge talked to me further about the idea of winning here. The bold talk of some startup carriers deriding the existing insurance industry may be missing something. He used the analogy of the tech boom of the late-1990s to illustrate his view on who will ultimately succeed. "The people who were really innovating at the time generally aren't here anymore. They ran out of cash or got acquired. But in the process, they forced the incumbents to get their stuff together."

If you look around at the innovative superstar startups of the day, the vast majority do not exist anymore, or at least not independently.

I was immediately reminded of how I used Alta Vista and Lycos to search the web on my Netscape browser, perhaps to find the name of a song to go search Napster for (not that I would have downloaded music illegally even if I found what I was looking for, of course) or to watch a sporting event on Quokka rather than ESPN or network TV. Literally none of these leaders exist today. And others that do exist are shadows of what they once were or promised to be. AOL and Yahoo are small units of Verizon. Monster.com, the job site that garnered so much attention for its Super Bowl ad in 1999 that cost more than their entire revenue for the year, is just a unit of staffing firm Randstad. The list goes on.

> "it's time for the industry to think more about how to make the CX really good and expand the perception of what we're offering."
>
> – Jeff Goldberg
> EVP of Research & Consulting, Novarica

Yet these disruptors did leave a mark. They disrupted their space and redefined the way many companies do business. Some of them still exist, though sometimes in different forms than they used to. Despite their disruption, the incumbents in markets with the dynamics insurance faces generally are still around, and have adapted to disruption by taking advantage of the tools and knowledge that disruption brought about.

With that in mind, Jeff Goldberg gives us a bit of positive self-talk around viewing ourselves as innovators. With all the hype around the subscription economy, he reminds us that insurance was the *original* subscription product. "One of the fascinating things about the new era of consumer products is that they're subscription-based. That's what insurance actually is – we're a subscription data and risk product, and have been forever." From that original point of being ahead of our time, Goldberg points to where we need to focus going forward when he advises, "it's time for the industry to think more about how to make the CX really good and expand the perception of what we're offering to be more than just billing and claims."

That is precisely where we are going to go next as we get into case studies from carriers who have evolved despite the headwinds all of us face. In each story, you will find a bit of guidance and inspiration that could help in the context you face at your own carrier.

II. THE NEXT EVOLUTION

As you think about what you are facing in your company, you may wonder how you can evolve to meet changing customer expectations and stave off the disruptive forces discussed in Part I.

Here, I share the stories of several carriers who have been able to evolve pieces of their business without massive investment, major disruption to customers (if any), employee revolt, competitors taking their market share, sparking market conduct exams by state DOIs, breaking the business in the process, or any of the other things we often fear. They were also able to do something everyone I've talked to brought up, moved their culture in the process.

In sharing these cases, it's important to know that these carriers aren't unique. By that, I mean they aren't immune to the headwinds discussed above. While they may not face all of the constraints and complications you face, they may face many others you are free from. At the end of the day, we are all operating in the same markets with similar dynamics at play. That means you can find inspiration in their examples that provide guidance as you think about how to move your business forward.

There are insights throughout these cases that have helped each of the carriers evolve in their given situation. A natural question you may have then is "Which one or ones should we do?"

In tackling this exact question in *The End of Insurance as We Know It*, Rob Galbraith went through four approaches or tools carriers can use: innovating within a traditional discipline like underwriting or claims; creating a "skunk works" or "lab" to generate and test out new ideas free from the core business; forming a separate, explicit innovation unit or team to find new solutions or solve problems within the business; create a venture capital arm to review insurtech solutions and form closer bonds with a select few; and then he added a fifth solution in the form of a blend of all of the above.

Ultimately, he settles on the ideal answer of, "it depends."[4] And he's right. There is no single, universal answer, so treat the insights, advice and lessons as input into figuring out the right path for your particular situation and needs.

I've structured the cases in a way that allows you to take in their story, hear how things have played out, and glean the key lessons. At the end of each case, you'll find a summary with key takeaway ideas from the case called "Foundations for The Future" listing some key factors that contributed to this being a case study in a positive outcome rather than one to use as a lesson in what not to do.

Each carrier learned something along their journey, and therein lies the real value of these cases. As I said earlier, I share none of them to give you a prescription for implementing a fraud or text messaging solution, for example. Instead, the point is to provide you with evidence of successful evolution in contexts that may resonate with what you face today. These key learnings are what we can all use going forward to break free of these headwinds we face and evolve.

I encourage you to take notes, think about your specific context in your carrier, consider how this case might apply to your context, and reflect on how the learnings and takeaways can impact what you are hoping to achieve. Talk about what you've read with a colleague, or boss or a peer and challenge yourself to see how you can evolve your world despite the barriers you are facing and the disruptive threats you may be under.

---

[4] Galbraith, pg. 297.

4. CSAA Insurance Group & Ride Sharing

In the early 2000s, I had a car that was recalled due to a wide-spread part failure which would render the car undrivable when it failed, which happened to me three times.[5] Each time, I was offered a loaner car by the dealer, but I couldn't use it because I lived in the city and couldn't park it on the street overnight. A loaner car would have lacked the prized-resident parking sticker that my own car had, giving access to free overnight street parking. The only way I could take the loaner car would be to pay to park it in a nearby garage for a big daily fee the manufacturer and dealer would not cover. Unfortunately, the dealer had no shuttle service, so I had to pay for a cab to take me to and from the dealership to drop off and pick up my car (since this was before ridesharing apps had been invented). Adding insult to injury, the dealer would not reimburse me for the cab ride since that was not an approved option from the manufacturer.

I even called the manufacturer's US customer support line to explain the situation and ask for reimbursement for a cab up to the cost of a rental, and they refused since it was not what the recall covered for transportation. Even though the cab cost less than the daily rental rate, they said they would not reimburse me. So, the "no-cost to our valued customers" recall ended up costing me over $100

---

[5] This story is from Volkswagen's Coil Pack Failure recall, which impacted over 500,000 cars globally, took months to sort out, and garnered the company much negative press. You can read more about it in this article from ConsumerAffairs.com: https://www.consumeraffairs.com/news03/vw_coils.html

out-of-pocket over the course of the three incidents.

If I had an insured loss where my car wasn't drivable, I would have faced the same situation. I had rental car coverage, but there was no consideration for situations like mine, where I couldn't actually have the rental overnight. I imagine I could appeal to my auto insurer as their intention is to make you whole in the event of a loss, and may have accommodated the parking fees, too.

In making an accommodation like this, my insurer would be making me happy, but increasing their loss cost in the process. Satisfied customers are great to have, but getting them by over-paying for claims is not a long-term winning strategy. If they had not done anything, I'd be unhappy as I would be paying for coverage I could not use. It's a lose-lose situation.

There is actually another potential issue brewing beyond higher-than-needed claims costs vs. lower-than-desired customer satisfaction – the potential end of human-driven cars as autonomy advances; potential shifting from Personal Auto insurance to Product Liability insurance that comes with AI-driven cars; and the possible end of individual car ownership all together. It may take a very long time for any of these things to become reality, and some may never fully play out, but development and movement toward each of these situations is already being made today. All of these dynamics pose a significant existential threat to an auto insurer, regardless of what a disruptive startup carrier might be doing.

In this context, enter CSAA Insurance Group, based in Walnut Creek, California, which provides AAA-branded insurance in twenty-three states plus Washington D.C. As a large auto insurer, rental car coverage is a common component to their claims. Adding to this, CSAA found that the majority of their Auto claims were fender benders where the car was still drivable, but required a two-to-three-day body shop visit.

That means the repairs are long enough repair cycles to be inconvenient for customers, but not long enough that customers would *necessarily* want to deal with getting a rental car. These customers would essentially find themselves in the situation I was in with my recall issue; not being able to take advantage of what they had paid for, being inconvenienced, and being out-of-pocket for expenses they probably feel they should not really be responsible for.

Traditionally, there is nothing a carrier can do since the coverage is for a rental car, and that customer, of their own free will, mind you, chose to forego that benefit despite paying for it. If customers did take the rental option, they may have gotten the value of their rental car coverage, but because of the added logistics of getting and returning the vehicle, the customer's satisfaction with the claim experience may fall below member expectations.

The only option for an insurance company is to leave the customer with an insured loss experience that is less-positive in their mind, right? Not an ideal answer.

Like many in the industry, CSAA works hard to reduce the perceived and actual challenge of getting a rental. That is, they had historically tried to improve the existing solution, without fundamentally changing it. They worked with their rental providers to increase the number of rental car offices that are collocated with or at least very near to preferred body shops and they instituted pick-up and drop-off options for those opting for rentals, etc. In the end, they found that people were still either not opting to get a rental in many covered cases, or were rating their experience below where CSAA hoped its customers would rate their satisfaction with their claim. It was clear that tweaks, although valuable, were not the complete solution.

If you think about renting a car, you can likely imagine why doing so may not lead to a totally positive claim experience. If you rent from an airport location (where most people do), you find a large inventory of cars, 24/7 operating hours, and a generally-smooth pick-up and return process. But most rentals for auto claims happen at local locations, not airports. These locations have many constraints the airport locations don't have. They have more limited hours, often opening too late for people's morning commutes or closing in the late afternoon when people may still be at work. They have far fewer cars to choose from, and less of a buffer of vehicles in case someone is late in returning one, or if there's a back-up of cleaning and preparing returned cars for a new renter since these locations have smaller lots and less volume to justify richer fleets. They also do not tend to have a small army of staff to keep the process moving for multiple customers at a time.

I rented from a local location recently and needed a pickup, only to find that the sole person working the customer counter also was the person who did my pickup, so she had to choose between locking the office while she came to get me and block potential customers from getting served, or pull their one vehicle prep person to handle the desk, meaning no cars would be made ready for rental while she was out getting me.

None of this is due to incompetence or not caring about customers, it's just a function of system constraints for understandable and unavoidable reasons. Despite that justification, if you had a car accident and had any delay or friction in getting a rental car, you would likely end up less-satisfied overall. That lower satisfaction is generally going to be directed at your insurance carrier, who you see as responsible for your total claim experience. Understandably.

With this context as the background in 2016, CSAA's relative new Strategy & Innovation team was tasked to identify innovative improvements in how the company does business. They turned internally to see what areas seemed to be causing friction or might serve as opportunities for improvement. Feedback from claims staff on the front lines had identified a number of opportunities, which included the rental experience.

The Strategy & Innovation team was created a few years ago, and is a great example of one of the ways to address innovation. You see several carriers putting resource behind the issue in different ways. Some will assign a long-standing leader with the task of heading "Innovation", but then not put much other resource or structure in place beyond that. As a result, the person may not be able to achieve much.

For CSAA, they set up a small, focused team to really dig into the issue as their full-time task, giving them different areas of focus within the team, so innovating across the entire business could be addressed. CSAA intentionally did not create the rest of the structure and processes around innovation, which led to some of the learnings we will discuss later in this case. Often it is important to figure out organically what is truly needed structurally to make innovation succeed by finding the bottlenecks in the processes as you work through it in your own organization.

> *"What if we look at what the customer is trying to do?"*
>
> – Brian Gaab
> Strategy & Innovation,
> CSAA Insurance Group

One of the original members of the Strategy & Innovation team is Brian Gaab. At the time, he was responsible for Core Innovation, meaning identifying and developing innovations in CSAA's core insurance business and working alongside the core business to bring those ideas to market. He started by taking the feedback from internal staff and added the external view of the rental car process to start thinking about the question.

The CSAA team asked a critical and different question than the industry had been asking in the past when looking at making the rental process smoother: "What if we stop thinking about this challenge through the lens of 'When a customer loses the use of their car, we give them another car to use.'? Instead, what if we look at what the customer is trying to do? They need to get from point A to point B. How do they do that today if they can't use their car?" Asking the question in this way can lead to completely new solutions.

The answer to this new question was simple – they used alternative transportation options, which increasingly included new mobility solutions like ride share apps, shared bikes and scooters, etc. Given CSAA's location in the Bay Area, the Innovation team tapped into its networks to connect with people at Lyft to talk about the issue and see if they would be interested in working on designing some possible solutions together. Lyft was curious, and agreed.

While many of us know and have used Lyft or their main rival, Uber, today, 2016 was still fairly early in the journey for ride share apps. To give you a sense of the difference in scale of ride sharing then versus today, Lyft had 3.5 million active riders at the beginning of 2016, and over 19 million at the beginning of 2019 around their IPO.[6] That is, less than 1% of the US population was using Lyft when CSAA talked to them, so it wasn't like this was a blatantly obvious answer to the 'Get from A to B' question.

The two firms talked about the idea, and problem-solved around what a solution could be. Gaab and the Claims team at CSAA collaborated with Lyft to better understand what a solution would need to look like to work for both the companies and their customers. Despite all their knowledge, and all the great customer and employee feedback the team had, there were a lot of unknowns that would be hard to answer without trying something in the real world because this was completely uncharted territory.

---

[6] Lyft S1 Filing, March 29, 2019.

While a traditional answer might have been to build out a full solution, work on the IT aspects to connect CSAA's claims core system with Lyft's backend, train all of CSAA's claims staff, announce something to customers and educate them, the teams from the two companies realized they needed to understand much more first, and wanted to find a way to do that without major investment, disruption or creating rigid solutions they would struggle to tweak and adjust as they learned more.

Once they got to that point, the Strategy & Innovation team presented the idea and others they had been working on to CSAA's Executive leadership. With this support, they got the green light to build a pilot of the idea to better understand what a production solution should really be before they expended any meaningful resources to build it or introduced any wide-spread risk to their business.

Next, Gaab and the team, built support and buy-in from the layers of people between the C-Suite and the line adjusters. This coalition-building was essential to ensuring success, as it provided more structure to the innovation process, enabled evaluation from across the business, and helped create knowledge and buy-in for approved projects.

Blindsiding people or leaving them out of the loop may exacerbate push back, and will not help an innovative idea succeed. In short, getting people aware, open and bought into new ideas like this is a step you cannot skip. While it may add time to your project, this culture work may just be one of the most important parts of any innovation you engage in.

With people across the organization aware and feeling like they are part of this new endeavor, the teams from the two companies got to work. Together, they designed what Gaab describes as low-fidelity a solution as possible. They started by deciding on the right place to pilot the idea. They had some opposing requirements. On one side, they needed enough volume to get meaningful feedback and data, but conversely, they needed to control the size and complexity of the pilot. This would also help protect the business at large from any risk from early wrong turns, while keeping the number of staff involved a manageable size to train and stay deeply engaged with throughout the pilot. One other wise choice was to limit sources of variability or unfamiliarity the team might have with the claims in the pilot, so they started with something they were all familiar with geographically – Northern California. They identified the adjusters handling those claims in CSAA's Colorado Springs call center as the pilot team, and started talking to them to make sure they were ready to try out the idea.

Initially, the project team wasn't sure who would and wouldn't take the option of using Lyft instead of getting a rental car, so they wanted to keep things open to the adjusters to make the decision of who to offer it to on a claim-by-claim basis. They had adjusters estimate the duration of the repair, and use that on which to base the decision to offer the Lyft option or not.

Next, they fixed the offering, rather than giving customers a variety of choices to scale with the severity of their loss, offering each customer the choice of up-to-$200 in Lyft credits or their rental coverage as-is. Customers could pick one or the other, but not a blend of the two options.

They put an expiration date on the credits, so that customers would not use them well-past the life of their claim, helping to control leakage and respecting the definition and regulation of indemnification, which allows for making a customer whole but not allowing them to profit from coverage.[7]

Logistically, CSAA got a set of voucher codes from Lyft with the parameters built in, and tracked the whole thing using a simple database. Again, the focus being on keeping it simple to put in place and manage while they were still learning.

The pilot was easy to setup, easy to track, and because it was kept in a tight roll-out area that still had sufficient scale, they could keep their arms around it in real-time to see how it was going and learn quickly.

Gaab and the Claims leadership team stayed close to the adjusters by being physically present in Colorado Springs, walking the floor, hearing from adjusters in real time.

After a few weeks, they moved to weekly meetings with supervisors to roll-up feedback and be more efficient in capturing it after early tweaks were made to make things smoother. They also realized that you need to keep line staff engaged and feeding back, so there was

---

[7] Merlin, Chip, "Can a Customer Profit from A Loss?" Merlin Law Group, December 3, 2019.

regular recognition for people who provided input.

Each company should think about what their teams are motivated by, and be open to using that to reward their early adopters and pilot staff for being committed to making innovation work. That includes engaging in ideas that end up not working in the end so people know it is good to try, learn and grow regardless of the immediate outcome as the evolution of the entire operation will not happen if people are afraid to take risks or only engage in the obvious wins. As the saying goes, baseball games are won through a mix of base hits and home runs.

Using this low-fidelity, grass-roots approach, CSAA and Lyft were able to play with many factors and solve for teething issues quickly.

They tried adjusting the dollar-value of the offer, the mechanism for giving the credits and more. They realized that they needed the ability to pull the credits back from a user's Lyft account if, for example, the customer realized they actually *did* need a rental car after taking the credits. They also found that adjusters sometimes allowed customers to take *both* options, given the specific circumstances of their claim. Sometimes, the rental really was right for the customer, but they needed help getting to the rental office. Or, perhaps they gave the rental back thinking their car was going to be ready that day, only to get a call from the body shop at the last minute to say they found an issue in the paint once it cured, and they need to keep it for another day. Suddenly having access to a ride from Lyft would solve an unforeseen "Getting from A to B" need the customer had that arose through no fault of their own.

This is the sort of thinking that would have helped in my story at the start of the case; solve the customer's need per your intended offer to help them while respecting your total cost expectations.

CSAA learned about customers in rural, suburban and urban settings, how they differ, and how what they chose differed from what was expected of them. This sort of customer insight is invaluable to companies.

For example, one finding that really surprised me came from people who lived in areas not yet served by Lyft since this was early in Lyft's life. Some of these people still chose the credits. That is, even when CSAA believed these people would never choose the credits because, on paper, they can't use them, the customers still did. Had CSAA only offered the credit option to people in urban areas, they would have missed this finding.

That means CSAA created a moment to make a customer happier than they would not have known about otherwise, and potentially even lower their loss cost by not giving an unneeded or un-valued rental car. Here, simplicity actually created opportunity and learning rather than limiting it, as we sometimes presume it will do.

Aside from things like this example of take-rates varying by demographics or other factors, CSAA was able to test the impact on customer satisfaction with the claim, and Net Promoter Score (NPS).[8]

For those who aren't familiar with NPS, it's a way of scoring a company based on percentages of customers who would promote your brand, be indifferent about it or actively tell people not to work with a given brand. It looks at people who score a company a nine or ten out of ten as Promoters, zero to six as Detractors and seven or eight as Passive. Your NPS is the percentage of Promoters minus the percentage of Detractors. In Auto Insurance, the industry NPS is thirty-nine,[9] with top performers above fifty, and plenty running in the teens. That is, it's a tough space to have high customer engagement.

High NPS is directly associated with higher customer retention, with Promoter retention nine points higher than Passive customers, and twenty-three points higher than Detractors. Think about what a point of retention is worth in your book of business.

At the scale of a carrier like CSAA, that can be tens of millions of dollars per year in retained business, per research done by Bain & Company, the creators of the NPS construct.[10] While CSAA does not share the impact on customer satisfaction or NPS publicly, they do confirm that they did indeed see a lift in NPS for those customers who were offered Lyft (no pun intended).

CSAA learned a great deal from the experiment, which allowed them to move forward in 2017 with a compelling offering on a national scale. That did not come overnight, though. The time from starting the pilot to going fully-live nationally took a year, with the go/no-go realization coming at the six-month mark after the pilot started. There

---

[8] "Introducing The Net Promoter Score," Bain & Company, December 8, 2011.
[9] "Average NPS of Selected Insurance Branches in the United States," Statistica, August 1, 2019.
[10] Bain & Company, 2011.

are various reasons for the time involved here, and Gaab believes they would have been able to move faster today.

Part of the time was simply due to not having the processes in place internally for approval and ongoing governance. Inventing it as you go can slow things down, but also allowed CSAA to ensure what processes and governance it did build would be sustainable, appropriate and helpful.

Another major factor was on the system side, both for CSAA and Lyft. For CSAA, to go into full production, they made a clear decision that this could not be a side-car solution running in a database tool, but instead had to live within their claims system. With the speed and volume of auto claims, expecting adjusters to be able to keep up with disparate systems, remember which customers took which offer in their heads, etc., was not a real option. Furthermore, sometimes, other adjusters or employees jump in on a claim and need to have the right information at their fingertips, which means it had to be in their claims system. Building the system connections took time, as there needed to be a way to connect their claims system to the APIs Lyft had built for the solution. While recent versions of many core claims administration systems are API-friendly, that wasn't always the case, so that work could be quite meaningful, and of course not every carrier is on a new-enough version of their own claims system to easily connect to APIs.

Speaking of Lyft's APIs to enable this, they didn't actually exist when the project started. Lyft built custom APIs for this project, which they did quickly and efficiently, but not as quickly or efficiently as they may be able to do today as they're a much larger and more mature company now than they were then. They also have a larger library of APIs they can pull from than they did back then. Their resources were more constrained, and they had several mission-critical projects going on that having tighter resources can make it hard to compete with for developer time. And, of course, the ride share market was not as developed as it is today, and no one had done this before, so a number of open questions had to be explored and answered before any of these bigger development efforts could be scoped and started.

After that year of work to go pilot, test, refine and build a production-level solution, CSAA's ride sharing offering today is a normal part of their (now perhaps mis-named) rental car coverage across their entire Auto book. Not only did they solve a real customer need the traditional thinking was consistently missing, they also moved the organization forward on how to look at questions like this and solve them in ways they would not have before.

CSAA's willingness to challenge itself, learn along the way, and design an organizational approach to the question of innovation has put them in a strong position as an innovator.

Today, they are working on a variety of new and interesting ideas around the question of mobility and what it means to be an Auto insurer given the shifting dynamics of how people drive, car ownership, and the new economy of people working in mobility in a way they never have before.

While they may have gotten to this place eventually without it, you can see how their work on this ride sharing question years ago set in motion an ability to tackle these bigger questions more effectively as an organization than they likely would have been able to otherwise.

Foundations for The Future

- Having people who are dedicated to innovation as their full-time role can help take ideas forward, but they need to have resources they can access and true executive support and sponsorship to be more than just a nice talking point in a company's annual report.

- To move past "how we've always done it", in the face of unmet customer needs, step back and ask what customers are trying to do. That question may have nothing to do with your company or your current offering. That's ok, and can lead you to outside ideas or approaches that make you more relevant and valuable to customers.

- Having buy-in across all layers and levels is important, not just C-Suite approval or line staff excitement; lacking this can make moving forward harder in the long run, so don't be afraid to invest in getting people aligned up front.

- Simpler, "low-fi" solutions can not only help you go live faster, but give you the space to learn and adjust in real time while also finding insightful surprises a more-engineered solution may preclude you from seeing.

5. CNA & Fraud

CNA is a storied brand in commercial lines. At well-over 100 years old, they are a company that has helped support global businesses through many major ups and downs. Given the lines of business they write, they are also one that has had to face the dilemma of actively battling fraud. In addition to the fraud found in Personal Auto, Property and Liability claims, which is mirrored in the commercial versions of those coverages CNA writes, their sizable book of Workers' Compensation (WC or Workers' Comp) business adds several additional sources of potential fraud.

Aside from the sort of "soft" fraud found in many claims where claimants may exaggerate losses to extract additional value from a claim, WC also faces many sources of "hard" fraud, including staged accidents and organized operations, where medical service providers collude with other bad actors to generate steady and sizable revenue streams from carrier claim departments.

CNA and similar companies have done a good job of making progress on dealing with fraud in WC and other lines, including using valuable partners in the fight against insurance fraud and crime like the National Insurance Crime Bureau (NICB) and in-house-developed fraud training and predictive models. All of these tools help in various ways, and have positive returns on investment in them.

Where these approaches can struggle is in their long-term impact. By this, I mean that the models that have been used were great at teaching newer claim handlers about what to look for in a claim to identify fraud. But because they are not dynamically adjusting to the shifting underlying characteristics of fraud and because they are not generally based on more modern and powerful algorithms, the marginal benefit of models starts to diminish for a handler as that handler gets more acclimated to the clear signs of fraud.

That is, models can serve as excellent training tools, but like any good student, eventually, the knowledge of the student may equal or even surpass the teacher, making the lessons less valuable.

Another issue many carriers face with existing fraud models is that they were not developed or deployed with an in-built ability to track the rate of false-positive results (claims flagged as having fraudulent activity that actually do not), making it hard to see how successful the models really are.

False-positives are an especially concerning issue for fraud models for two reasons. First, they result in a less-efficient Special Investigations Unit (SIU) since the team ends up reviewing cases where there is no actual cause for alarm, taking from their capacity to investigate genuine cases of fraud.

Second, you can create a "boy who cried wolf" problem where people think the model is over-zealous, so they can just ignore when it flags a case. Imagine how you'd react when the last five claims you have touched are all flagged as having potential fraud, get investigated, and all get cleared by the SIU? Do you think you would pay attention to the sixth claim in a row? Or any after that one for that matter (except perhaps the most blatant ones)? In this way, you may actually undo the educational value of that model over time as you end up desensitizing claim handlers to fraud.

Lastly, because these models also were generally not made to track the value or accuracy of the valid positive cases flagged, it is difficult to see the true worth of the solution or whether it was worth further investment in the models. That is, you struggle to track the total dollar amount of reduced fraudulent payments as a result of the model flagging claims for potential fraud.

This is the situation CNA was in when Rob Thomas, Senior Vice President of Claim Analytics, Finance & Operations, joined CNA's Worldwide Claim team in July 2017. His broad functional remit included looking at CNA Claim's state of analytics and determining where to focus going forward.

Analytics are an especially powerful tool to help gain clarity into more effectively combating fraud while increasing the success of recovery and subrogation activities. In addition to other valuable efforts to drive increases in customer satisfaction, retention, etc., improving the SIU's suite of tools aligned well with the goals of the Claim organization more broadly. As a result, this is where Thomas started.

He went back to his Analytics team to see what resources they had to address the question of improving CNA's ability to root out fraud. He asked a few basic questions to assess the right path, including:

- What models do we want to build?
- What's the priority of these models?
- What's the expertise and capacity we have in-house such that the models we build would be great?

What he found was clarity around the need to look at the predictive fraud tools, but his Data Science team lacked specific expertise in fraud. He then looked to the SIU team to see if they had any model-building skills amongst their fraud experts, and found that they did not. This meant CNA lacked an in-house, fraud-savvy data scientist, which is what would be needed to work on this question themselves. This made having an advanced, predictive fraud tool built was a prime candidate for outsourcing.

CNA had several options at their disposal outside the company. Many consulting and actuarial sciences companies have built up strong practices in the predictive analytics area, with fraud being a common theme for projects. I myself had looked at several of them while running Claims at Hiscox. And they do excellent work. However, the approach is generally to build a model based on your data that is then left behind for you to run without ever updating, figure out how to update yourself as fraud patterns in the data change, or re-engage the consultant periodically to freshen the model.

There's nothing inherently wrong with that approach, but given that Thomas had already determined they did not have the right skill set at CNA, self-administering the tool was not the solution he was after. Lacking dynamic improvements in the model further concerned him as the model's ability to keep up with the way fraud patterns change is critical. As those committing fraud get savvier as they learn how to avoid detection by traditional methods, Thomas wanted to ensure their model adjusted, too.

The other reason Thomas was particularly interested in a different path was that he realized the industry as a whole sees fraud, not just CNA. That means there is far more insight that could be incorporated from a partner with an industry-wide viewpoint, rather than one built off the experience of just one insurer.

Thomas sees fighting fraud as a common good rather than a

competitive tool (though of course it can allow you to price more aggressively if you are better at avoiding fraud than a competitor). Indeed, this idea is the reason why the NICB exists as a cross-industry, non-profit organization. As Thomas put it, CNA may have seen a lot of fraudulent scenarios, but if it comes across one it has never seen before, a model based only on their data would never capture that. But if the model is built by a partner with a broader knowledge base, it will contemplate nuances of fraud CNA might have missed.

All of this helped Rob Thomas and his team get clarity on what exactly they needed to look for, which was ultimately an expert in fraud *specifically* that can keep learning through broad experience. They wanted a partner who would work with the right third-party resources, like the NICB, so CNA did not also have to manage various ways to enrich the model. That lead them to Shift Technology in August 2017, a French data science solution that was laser-focused on fraud with many successful, large-scale deployments from top global carriers.

> "Shift understands that the true power of artificial intelligence is to arm people with incredible decision support capabilities."
>
> – Jérémy Jawish
> Co-Founder & CEO,

There was one problem, though. Shift had never worked in the US market. While you might presume fraud is fraud, there are certainly differences by geography, impacted by things such as local regulation, how healthcare works in a given market, quality of law enforcement, severity of penalties for insurance fraud, and other factors.

What helped CNA get comfort with Shift and to be willing to take a risk despite the lack of US experience was Shift's vision around fraud. It mirrored what CNA had flagged as the reasons to look outside the company and outside the consulting company approach. Like CNA, Shift also sees fighting fraud as a common good, and because they were data scientists who understood fraud, they would have the combined expertise and business understanding CNA had tried to find in-house.

Shift co-founder and CEO, Jérémy Jawish, explained their vision in more detail:

"In addition to being laser-focused on the insurance industry, Shift also understands that the true power of artificial intelligence is to arm people with incredible decision support capabilities. We're not the arbiter of whether fraud occurred or not. It's not the computer's job to say definitively whether or not a claim is fraudulent or whether it's legitimate. It's to look at all the evidence, all the data, in a way that's impossible for a single human being to do, and make a highly educated assessment of the claim. Not whether the claim is suspicious or not, but how suspicious is the claim and why? After that, human claim handlers with years of experience are better able to make the final determination."

After considering several options, CNA decided to move forward with Shift. From their initial meeting in 2017, they started working on an agreement and did the vendor management and IT security vetting starting in Q1 2018. The i-dotting and t-crossing was complete by mid-summer, with the first dataset being sent to Shift in late-July.

While this timetable may sound stereotypically-long for the insurance industry in its length, things changed dramatically once the procedural pieces of the puzzle were solved. While we may wish we could short circuit that upfront part of the process, Thomas is quick to remind us that we cannot put the company at risk just because we may think we have the answer or because we like a given solution.

While CNA was already comfortable with cloud-based SaaS solutions at this point, it was still Shift's first US deployment, and in today's cyber-crime and regulatory environment, you cannot simply skip the security assessment stage.

Thomas had the support of the senior executives and the new Global Head of SIU, but he was also new to CNA and still appreciated what was at stake for the company if this decision was wrong. Remember, when you say a claim is fraudulent, the additional effort of investigating for fraud may lengthen the overall handling time, so the experience for the insured or injured party could be negatively impacted. If you are wrong about there being fraud (a false-positive), you could be making a bad situation in someone's life worse by taking more time to resolve the matter. It is not simply about not wanting to waste the SIU's effort on a false-positive, but also an issue of respecting the situation for the injured worker, and their desire to be well again as quickly as possible.

So, you do not merely say yes because it is a neat solution, but you also do not just say no because it is new, different, has risk, etc. This is an important idea to keep in mind, especially in the insurance industry where not just saying no to new ways of working is perhaps the biggest headwind we face when looking at innovation.

Once the checks, balances and controls had been done, it was time to move forward.

CNA had a cross-functional team assembled within its Claim organization to work with Shift. Thomas's Vendor Management team had felt a need for a project manager on the CNA-side to oversee the project given the tight timing Shift had proposed of a three-month cycle. Additionally, they would need people from the SIU to give the subject matter expertise and guidance to Shift; data scientists and IT to ensure Shift was really delivering what they said they would (we have all seen vendors who talk a great game, but when you look behind the curtain, you find they are not really delivering what they promised) and CNA's Office of Change Management & Training to ensure the staff would be ready for the change.

There would be changes in how SIU worked since the investigators would be seeing something different, and CNA setup a Triage function in SIU to look at the model-referred cases, so SIU was an obvious candidate for Change Management's attention. However, there was also a need to train and manage change in the broader Claim organization.

This last part was particularly crucial, and not one you may think you would need since looking at fraud was not a new idea, and the SIU would be performing the same function they had been performing before in terms of investigating flagged claims. Thomas used a great analogy around how much operational change you may really be asking of people despite the theme being constant.

If you are a mechanic working on family sedans for twenty years and then someone brings a diesel-powered semi-truck in for repairs, it is still an automobile, but there are some material differences in what you are seeing (especially in the way the engine works) that do require training to handle.

Interestingly, this was a source of unforeseen benefit for CNA. The training around the new fraud tool instantly raised awareness around the subject of fraud throughout the Claim organization. Handlers who had not been thinking about fraud suddenly had it on the top of their mind, so CNA saw an increase in referrals of quality cases to the SIU before Shift's tool even went live. And after Shift went live, they found that handlers had a healthy competitive drive to "beat the model", so this vigilance stayed up even after the newness faded. Thomas refers to this as a "sentinel effect", with everyone standing guard.

Getting into the project, with the right people in place on both sides, Shift and CNA agreed to start with Auto claims, which should be a bit easier to begin with than Workers' Compensation due to a simpler set of situations and drivers, and more alignment with Shift's past work in Europe. After getting data from CNA in July, Shift took 100 cases to run through their initial model. At the end of the first month, Shift came back with results. The two companies' teams met to review each case, with the three to four CNA SIU investigators feeding back to Shift which cases they agreed with, which they did not (false-positives), and what other changes they might suggest to the modelers.

Shift took the feedback into account, adjusted the model, and ran through another 100 cases. This time, rather than going case-by-case in person, CNA realized they could split the caseload amongst the SIU team ahead of time and be more productive in the meeting. They held the second review at the end of month two following the same concept of guiding Shift on false-positives, valid fraud flags, and other general feedback on the results.

One thing the two teams worked on throughout this process was the reason codes Shift presented when it flagged fraud. Unlike CNA's legacy model or handler-flagged cases, Shift did not just say, "This case seems to have fraud." The Shift model actually went beyond flagging and gave explanations of what it was finding so investigators knew more specifically what to look for, as Jawish described as part of their philosophy above. This allowed cases flagged by Shift to be investigated faster than before, creating an unforeseen efficiency and effectiveness in the SIU team.

After the two proof-of-concept test-and-adjust runs of the model, a final model was shown in October 2018, the third month of the Auto Claims model development. CNA was satisfied with the results of that model, and they were able to go live in full production, and kicked off their training and change processes, allowing for full deployment in early January.

I think this kind of development and deployment speed would impress many of us in the industry given past experiences. This is a point I found first hand while working on deployments with Hi Marley; we expect talk of how long it takes to go live to be half-true (at best). That is, a vendor or provider says it will take three months, and we think it will be more like six-to-eight, or longer. While there are certainly plenty of examples like that around today, there are now many examples like what Shift or Hi Marley are able to do in terms of fast, on-time deployment.

Thomas shared that the Shift program was the only one on CNA Claim's project dashboard he was managing that had been green for delivery the entire time. What I have not shared yet that makes this even more impressive is that Shift was not just working on the Auto model during that time. After working on Auto for a month, they decided to start the Workers' Compensation model, so they actually had two concurrent Shift projects that were green throughout their lifecycle on the project dashboard.

Everything sounds good up to this point, but we have not talked about results. First, as I mentioned above, there was this sentinel effect Thomas described, resulting in more referrals to SIU overall, whether from the model or claim handlers. That means CNA was increasing its chances of catching fraud. This is a good thing, and yet could also mean the SIU would be slammed with excess work, and either miss things or need to staff up, perhaps so much that it negates any savings from catching that fraud. What CNA found is that, aside from adding the triage function, the SIU staffing has not been impacted by the change. Yes, caseloads are higher per investigator, but each investigator is more efficient because of the richer information they have when a claim is referred, allowing them to be more laser-focused in their investigation.

Additionally, fraud is being caught earlier. Catching fraud after you have paid for something you should not have paid for means you may never see that money again, since you would be trying to get someone dishonest and/or malicious to pay you back. And even if they want to, the money may be long gone, so they simply cannot pay you back.

When you catch fraud earlier, you increase the chance of not making fraudulent payments at all, eliminating the need to chase the fraudulent actors for recoveries after the fact. Traditionally, claim handlers may diarize checking on cases every thirty days, for example.

If bad actors are committing fraud within that time period, no one would know they had a case to refer to SIU until after a payment was made or the thirty-day check-in had been done. Shift's model is analyzing claims every day starting at first notice of loss, meaning CNA can catch fraud earlier than ever before. In fact, they have seen a sixty-day average improvement in speed to refer a claim to SIU, which is material when you realize an injury claim may be open for six months or longer. In that context, a two-month-faster referral is profound.

Another benefit CNA has realized is exactly what they were hoping for when they chose to look for an outside solution dedicated to fraud, noticing patterns and situations they would not see themselves. They started to spot patterns that were too nuanced or non-obvious for individuals to identify. It also allowed them to see aggregation of fraud activities from specific providers no claim handler, or even team of handlers, would be able to spot because they lack a global view of all activity with a provider over time each time they are presented with a bill to pay.

For example, a given injury may generally take four to five visits to get an injured worker healed and back to work. A provider may systematically be taking five to seven visits on average, throwing in a random three-or-four-visit-claim now and then to keep from looking suspicious (for example, doing it the second time the same handler has a claim with that provider to avoid raising suspicion). People would not generally spot this kind of pattern, but a model that looks across everyone, that is also informed by behaviors seen in the experience of every carrier on the platform will notice these patterns. That may save you from paying that next fraudulent bill, but more importantly, it allows you as a carrier to direct cases away from that provider to stop from ever being at risk of being defrauded by them again.

This may sound far-fetched to some who have not been in the WC or bodily-injury space, or perhaps it sounds like paranoia that there are providers acting in this way, when the overwhelming majority of doctors and therapists genuinely want to help people get healthy and stay that way while doing no harm, per the Hippocratic Oath.

Despite this being rare, unfortunately, there are pockets of individuals behaving this way, as SIU investigators and experts at the

NICB can attest to.[11]

Thomas shared evidence that this is not just paranoid or overly-cost-conscious insurers worrying. Some practitioners who have been flagged of behaving in this way actually have been found to have lists in their offices of which insurers not to accept claims from as those carriers are wise to the game. Fraud like this is not just hurting insurers, but injured workers, too. Needing more treatments is not necessarily a good thing. When you are injured, you really just want to be healthy and getting back to living your life, not having to go to another appointment while you are still in pain.

Another form of benefit CNA saw is in a situation specific to Workers' Compensation insurance called compensability.[12] This is when the accident did in fact occur, and the severity and costs are genuine. However, the accident occurred outside of the coverage period, for example just before the person was employed with the company or perhaps before they showed up for work that day (like getting hurt at home before coming in). CNA had no intention of Shift looking at the compensability question, but it was so good at spotting it that they were able to expand its use to address that issue, too.

I asked about the loss ratio impact or the saved dollars from using Shift, which is harder to answer.

That is not because it was deployed lacking the ability to look at this question (as we had discussed earlier around the legacy tools being used). The issue here is merely one of time lag. If a claim with fraud is open for nine to twelve months (a little longer than the average claim), and medical billing is not instantaneous, you can see that it may take a little over a year to start to get a sense of the bottom-line savings from Shift.

As of the writing of this case, CNA had only just past the one-year mark on the platform, so they have not quite seen enough data yet. The tools are in place to measure this, and the consensus sentiment in the company is that it is saving them real money because it helps CNA pay what is truly owed for a claim, while making their SIU resources even more efficient and effective.

---

[11] National Insurance Crime Bureau Blog, "Winners & Losers"
[12] For a more complete understanding of Compensability, please see this definition from USLegal.com: https://definitions.uslegal.com/c/compensable-injury/

Aside from the benefits Thomas shared, he added a point about integration. Shift has a web-based tool the SIU team accesses each day in their triage process and then when an investigator looks into a matter referred to them by triage. I asked why it was not integrated into Guidewire ClaimsCenter, which CNA uses as its core claims system.

There were a few reasons for this. First, while Shift has a Guidewire Accelerator to ease integration, it does not replicate all of the richness of their standalone web-based tool, which Thomas noted is particularly good in its ease-of-use and richness of information. There would be a cost to using the Accelerator, even if it was small, and the fact that there is also functionality cost to integrating, it was not worth taking IT resources for that work over other Guidewire enhancements CNA was interested in.

Second, Thomas noted that their SIU and handler teams had not used a fraud tool like this before. Taking something totally new and shoving it into their work flow without the critical thought process of the triage function would likely lead to more false-positives. That would just put more work on the SIU team that did not yield value, and it would likely mean people would not trust the output as much, leading to the "boy who cried wolf" issue they were trying to avoid.

While the project is still going on (they were adding Commercial Property to the mix as this book was being written), CNA has been very happy with the results of their decision. It was a big risk in many ways, given that Shift had no US experience, and the reputational-, regulatory- and SIU-efficacy threats were very real. Despite all of that, not simply saying no in the face of those concerns allowed CNA to push the envelope and be a first-mover in their market with something their Claim organization has truly embraced and the company sees as a very positive addition to their ability to manage their risk and thrive.

As Rob Thomas shared, "We wanted to signal that you can, as a 120-plus-year-old company, be current, change how you operate, successfully integrate a third-party vendor from France to use an AI-powered solution…it wasn't about just getting the model, but sending the signal to change the culture."

Foundations for The Future

- While it is important to do your due diligence and be mindful of things like Information Security, it is just as important not to simply say no in the face of changing things you have never changed or doing something different to how you've operated in the past. This may be the hardest change of any evolution insurers do.

- Having an engaged, cross-functional team from the start helps build a coalition of support across all impacted teams so that you can tackle the change management from a more informed and inclusive place than you might with a more siloed approach.

- Be open to what you do not know as you may find benefits you never expected, but not if you have preemptively closed the door to the potential of that happening, as CNA saw with compensability and finding patterns in medical provider practices they would have otherwise missed.

6. State Compensation Insurance Fund & Online Quote & Bind

I've discussed the headwinds we face as an industry, and noted how we do not all face the same headwinds, or one carrier may face the same ones to different degrees than another carrier might.

The State Compensation Insurance Fund of California (SCIF) faces headwinds most carriers would never stop to think about. As a governmental agency, an additional layer of potential complexities and unique workforce-related dynamics get added into the SCIF context (for example, SCIF has civil servants and union staff members, which few other carriers, if any, face; this is not a problem per se, but presents considerations many carriers would not have to account for); and other requirements like needing to choose California-based partners, all else being equal, when they look at utilizing new technology or services from vendors. And those are just some of the added nuances to the SCIF story.

SCIF started, as many state fund carriers do, as a single-state, mono-line, Workers' Compensation market-of-last-resort. They typically held about 20% of the WC market in California, providing coverage to companies that couldn't find it elsewhere or at least had a very hard time securing coverage at a reasonable rate.

SCIF's business was fairly balanced between business from the residual market (where they served as the market-of-last-resort) and other business. State funds like SCIF have helped keep state economies moving by allowing businesses to operate with the protection and space commercial insurance aims to provide. Many of them still operate today, though often in different capacities than those in which they were founded, like the various medical malpractice carriers that were setup in the 1970s and 1980s that now operate as commercial enterprises.

In the wake of some regulatory changes and developments in the tail of past years of account plus trends in newer years, things shifted in the California Workers' Compensation market. Suddenly, carriers that had been open to providing Workers' Compensation coverage in California tightened up their appetites, or shut the state off completely for new business while making renewing unattractive or onerous, driving a surge in the size of the residual market SCIF was created to serve.

I remember being at Liberty Mutual at the time, and seeing how we pulled back from our acquisition of Golden Eagle Insurance to expand our California WC book in response to these dynamics shifting. We literally walked away from a strategic acquisition of a nearly-$1-billion carrier because of the state of the market in California, if that gives you a sense of the scale and speed of change at the time.

Suddenly, SCIF had a fifty-percent-or-more share of the California market, and rocketed to being the largest comp carrier in the *country*. And this all happened rapidly, practically overnight by insurance standards.

With that shift in market share, SCIF's capital ballooned to over $30 billion, with nearly half of that sitting in reserves. It also meant they could no longer exist as a carrier that did not need to be concerned with being profitable given the scale of the losses that could hit the state. That is, its remit as a market-of-last-resort was no longer a viable model. It was time for SCIF to become competitive, or risk taking down one of the largest economies in the world along with itself.

Despite the growth in the size of the business, SCIF was still operating like a market-of-last-resort. That is, they were not providing industry-leading customer or broker service, and were operating on top of outdated systems and processes. As we get deeper into this case, you will see examples of this in action in the discussion of the quoting and binding processes. Because of this, as soon as commercial carriers decided to re-enter the California Comp market meaningfully, SCIF went from being larger than ever to the smallest they have ever been by 2011 at under 10% market share, and were no-longer balanced between regular and residual market business. That is to say, SCIF grew because employers had no choice but to get coverage from SCIF rather than because they actually wanted to. As soon as choice returned, these businesses fled in droves because SCIF was not meeting customers' needs well enough to warrant renewing with them.

In 2014, with a new CEO, Vern Steiner, the company realized they must change, becoming a carrier with a customer experience that actually leads to employers choosing to be covered by SCIF. This was really a recognition of the need to change from doing business the way they used to when profitability was not necessary. That meant that SCIF would need to seek out new ways of delivering underwriting and claims service, work with medical providers, and more.

That sort of change can be very hard on staff at any company, and unions in many industries have been wise to be concerned that automation of processes can threaten employment levels.

SCIF, despite having some unionized and some civil servant staff, engaged with their employees collaboratively, in a way that set the tone for people being supportive of change and helping SCIF do it right. This was a lesson in how the right engagement with people that is open, honest and inclusive is critical to successful evolution, regardless of the structure or organizational relationship employees have to their employer.

Steiner commented on this directly when he spoke about how the company engaged with its people, seeing the nuances to the types of employees they had as a mechanism to remember to be more thoughtful:

"The way I generally approach this topic is to give credit to the structure. We are constrained by rules that arise from both civil service and unions. While that can make it more difficult to move quickly with a top down approach, it actually encourages us to engage with our people more, which has led to more sustainable change than if it were rushed or forced on the organization.

Honestly, we would have done it the same way regardless of the structure, but I do believe that the structure requires us to use higher level leadership skills that are more effective long term."

To start to change, and do so in a way that brought the entire organization along, the executive team got together in September 2015 to set a strategy. They saw that they were saddled by many legacy system constraints, were rolling out new systems to overcome them and catch up to the market, but weren't thinking about how to thrive beyond that. It was like being behind in a race, seeing the pack up ahead, and thinking you can just run to where they are in that moment without contemplating how they would be further ahead by the time you got there.

SCIF's leadership took two approaches. They identified two major, strategic shifts themselves (more on these in a moment), while creating an organization that could identify and rapidly implement other changes. This balanced their ability to evolve across the spectrum and scale of issues they faced, while also getting the entire employee base meaningfully engaged in innovation.

The employee-driven change, in the eyes of CEO Steiner, is how you ensure long-term innovation through creating a truly innovative culture. Doing one successful project won't actually keep them thriving long term, and SCIF realized this.

In 2018, Steiner went to their Training and Development team to task them with how to make innovation a part of their DNA. The team developed something they call "Experiences by Design." It's a program based on Design Thinking where they run sessions centered around a problem statement. The participants then develop a suggested solution, test it rapidly and see what would work. They put the entire company through these programs so no one was left out of the shift in mindset and how to make it reality.

Steiner and the T&D team knew merely putting people through the exercise was not good enough, and if the ideas ultimately went nowhere, it would signal to the staff that SCIF was just talking about evolving, but not serious about it. On the back of the program, they then ran a number of design thinking problem challenges where winning ideas from each challenge would be chosen.

Thirty-one challenge-winning ideas were found, which is an astoundingly large number. To show they were genuinely valuable and SCIF was serious, eighteen of these ideas were being implemented as of early 2020.

And yet they did not stop there. Recognizing everyone has a day job, and can't keep being pulled out of it for challenges, in late Q1, Steiner and his team established an innovation function and a design center with a full-time leader of innovation named. When a functional team comes up with a problem, they can take it to the Innovation and Design Team to find a way to solve it using design thinking. The team runs a ninety-day cycle to come back to the business owner with a proposed solution to be tested and piloted, with some of the early projects already in testing.

Through the Experiences by Design and the new Innovation and Design Team, SCIF has created a strong, bottom-up, culture shift around evolving throughout its future. That still leaves ensuring the leadership of the company has its eye on big, strategic questions going forward.

To that end, the leadership team set aside time to think about not just where the world is, but where it is going. It was a case of the famous Wayne Gretzky quote of skating to where the puck would be.

There were two major issues they had identified and started working on. One is around truly revolutionizing the claim process for insureds, injured workers and medical providers that is called UR Connected, which SCIF is rolling out as this case is being written. The other major theme, and the focus of this case, is around the notion of the "Amazonification" of buying going on across industries.

People were becoming not just comfortable with, but actually *expectant* of simple, digital, direct purchasing options for increasingly complex products and services.

Personal Lines experienced a huge shift online in the early 2000s, but Commercial Lines like WC never seemed to be able to catch on in the same way. It's understandable when you think about the additional complexity of commercial coverage over personal lines, but also because the underwriting has always been far more involved.

Rare exceptions, such as Hiscox USA's successful small business direct offering or the recent push by Berkshire Hathaway with biBerk and Three are still tiny as compared to the broader commercial market. Buyers need help understanding what to get, and also how to complete applications, which can feature well-over fifty or even 100 questions.

At the time the executive team started talking about it in 2017, SCIF would ask a small business looking for coverage eighty-eight questions to complete their submission to underwriting, who would then potentially have more questions to generate a quote; daunting for any insured, and certainly not the kind of thing you'd want to do without the help of a licensed broker or agent.

In fact, this is where the innovation really came to play. When you hear about offering quotes or binding coverage online, you may think it's a technology question. You need a web interface that talks to your core system, connects to your rating engine, has the human decision capabilities turned into an algorithm, can do real-time document generation, etc. While those capabilities are important, that is not really what SCIF had to innovate on to make their vision a reality. In fact, that aspect was fairly trivial for their IT team given the work SCIF had already done to modernize their systems.

Instead, the trick was in changing the way this 105-year-old (at the time) organization thought about how it evaluated risk. Each of those eighty-eight new business underwriting questions they asked had years, perhaps even decades of justification behind needing to ask for that information. Underwriters and Actuaries had stood by the rating impact of every factor, and taking away even a small piece of the picture of that risk they had established over the years triggered the kind of risk aversion our industry can be known for.

Heading up the task was Dante Robinson, who was the Chief of Internal Affairs, including functions like the SIU and Internal Audit. This background gave Robinson not only a broad view of the business, but the mindset to ask questions and seek out underlying or hidden answers that could unlock something meaningful for SCIF. It also meant he was not directly living in the midst of these eighty-eight questions, so he was free of any longstanding history of feeling the need to ask them.

What SCIF realized is that, to serve customers directly starts with a completely different mindset from their broker business. They had been serving direct customers as they did brokers before. They described the difference as customers thinking, "help me," and brokers thinking, "transact me". Customers need guidance, clarity and transactions whereas brokers are interested in getting the transaction done as they have clarity themselves and don't need guidance.

Recognizing this very different mentality, Steiner challenged his team. They were talking about small accounts (up to $25,000 in premium), and likely new businesses that had never bought coverage before. They saw this group as the most likely to shop direct, online.

It also meant the risks were simpler, smaller and would not have answers to many underwriting questions that a company with decades of loss history data might. He told his team SCIF would not ask a single question they did not absolutely need, and had the group go through each question, one by one. From eighty-eight questions, they only were able to remove ten to twenty this way, not enough to cut it.

Steiner challenged his team to push harder. Robinson had brought Cameron Anthony, a SCIF veteran of sixteen years, into the team as project manager to oversee delivery of the project and work with Accenture on a three-month effort to define requirements for this new direct play.

> "This is about establishing the relationship the customer needs rather than the relationship we need."
>
> – Cameron Anthony Program Manager, State Compensation Insurance Fund of California

Through a series of intense workshops, Anthony, Accenture and representatives from Underwriting met to take on Vern Steiner's challenge to reduce the questions free of the legacy mindset of, "You can't do that!" that is embedded in many carriers' culture, SCIF included. Instead of testing each of the remaining questions, they took a more clean-sheet approach to create a set of data they absolutely had to know to rate the risk, and nothing more. As Anthony put it, "You don't make change by rebuilding what's there."

What they found was a series of long-lived interpretations that had become the rules of the way that may not actually be accurate. They challenged each of them to see if it was a mandated rule or regulation, or if it was internal perception of a need that isn't really necessary. To put it more simply, they asked, "Why?" Asking this is important to obtaining the understanding for the need rather than simply cutting or keeping a question blindly.

As an example, the California State Licensing Board (CSLB) required anyone doing construction work in the state to carry a license. SCIF had been collecting the license information during the quoting process as a courtesy to CSLB, but it had no bearing on the rate or insurability of the risk. If no license was provided in the submission, SCIF would not offer a quote as it was deemed to be an incomplete submission and would be closed out, meaning the prospect put in the effort to complete the application for nothing.

Anthony and the team asked, "Why are we asking for information that does not impact pricing or help the insured make a decision about buying the policy?"

As a result of this and other, similar challenges Underwriting, Anthony and the rest of the team made of how they had been doing business, they were able to bring the question set down dramatically. It was a collaborative process that took everyone being open to thinking differently that was yielding dramatic improvements to the submission and quoting processes.

To build a new set of questions, they asked, "What would a customer need to tell us about themselves for us to know what they do?" This is a nuanced difference from the more traditional, "What do we need to ask customers for our needs?" It was about a shift in perspective allowing for fresh thinking around an old problem. Anthony said it well, "This is about establishing the relationship the customer needed rather than the relationship we needed."

Some work they had done the year before helped. SCIF had been verifying the information in all applications before quoting. While they enjoyed a very high hit rate of 40%, that still meant they were wasting effort on 60% of all submissions. They started to quote as if the data in the submission was accurate, and then would verify pre-bind if the quote was accepted. This protected them from being on risk if there was an issue while allowing for efficiency and faster turnaround time for prospects to get a quote. That experience showed them detail on what data tended to be accurate or not, where people may misrepresent themselves, and how some questions ended up not impacting the final underwriting decision (since verifying the information didn't change the outcome).

What if they could assume more of the answers were valid and within reason for a competitive quote?

They could still check afterward using other data sources, but could that approach allow them to cut additional questions? They ended up getting to a final question set of just *sixteen* questions on average to get a quote (and a maximum of just seventeen), with up to just five more questions to bind. Since some questions are triggered by your answers to others, the number can vary. That said, the *most* a customer might answer is twenty-three. They've had customers go through the entire process in just three-and-a-half-minutes.

It's valuable to pause here and compare this to how things used to work.

With the old eighty-eight-question application, SCIF would also run what's called a Pre-Coverage Check to see if the insured had an outstanding balance. They would also check that the Broker of Record was licensed and had an agreement in place. This took a-day-and-a-half to two days on average, and up to five after the customer had made it through all of their questions. The quote might take another two to five days to go out, depending on the need for any follow up questions, and the speed of the customer and SCIF to correspond through that back-and-forth process. If the customer decided to bind, they would have to send in a paper check to SCIF to move forward. Depending on the customer's location in the state and the speed of service they used to mail in the check, this might add three days or more. Coverage would then only be bound only as soon as the day after the check was received by SCIF. Obviously, the new approach was dramatically different, and sounds likely to succeed just on the speed and ease of business improvements, let alone being a more modern interaction customers sought.

With this new, streamlined small business application, SCIF moved forward with putting the tool out in the market. They released it to the public with no fanfare or marketing on October 26, 2019.

While it was live, something was not quite right. The team found some hiccups around getting complete process to work, and stayed late into the night working on things, finally going home around 3 a.m. While testing the next morning, a customer got into the system and got through the process, and bound a policy. The team didn't think this was possible since they thought the system was still down, but the customer apparently found a way in. This was a Sunday, which may have been the fist-time they bound a policy on a Sunday in SCIF's existence.

By November, still with no marketing, bound policies through the direct channel increased 92% from the prior year and premium was up 60%. Then, still with no marketing, December premium rose 50% from the year before. In January, they did some light online advertising, and saw premium increase 144% from a year earlier to over two-and-a-half million dollars. In February, the trend continued, with another more-than-doubling of the prior-year's premium. They had a goal of seeing 98% of small business activity going through the Direct Quote and Bind solution, and hit that number in February.

While the prior year numbers they were growing from were small, they still created a more-than-$25 million run rate business, and did it without adding more staff to do any of this. They merely challenged and changed the way they looked at how they did business.

Through the process, they also learned some things about these customers, and how they're different.

Brokers tend to send in business during the first week of the month, so you can get a feel for your whole month's production quickly, and manage capacity consistently. With these new, direct customers, SCIF found that they buy insurance when they needed rather than based on someone else's calendar. SCIF might see a big day, then volume falls off, then it jumps back up again. They see customers looking for coverage all hours of the day and night, on weekends and even on Thanksgiving and Christmas (which they found are days people do in fact look for insurance coverage). Being able to be responsive and fast allows them to capture this opportunity whenever it arises.

While SCIF had been a direct writer earlier in its life, its focused had shifted to establishing and nurturing broker relationships through its competitive years, which resulted in neglecting their direct book of business. The investment in Quote and Bind was more than just a shift to online sales, but a way of addressing the unique needs of its direct customers.

Its direct business still existed, but did minimal volume. Now it was starting to generate meaningful new business activity, which could be seen as creating channel conflict or a threat to its broker business. Adding to that, the price is 6% lower for direct-sold policies due to the lower expense load in the rating.

However, what SCIF found is that this is a market segment that some brokers aren't inherently focusing on today. Because premium is low, commissions are not often sufficient to justify the time a broker spends to service the business, making it an unattractive focus area for their efforts. And if an insured looking for a larger policy were to come through the direct channel, they would not qualify for the simpler question set, and would likely seek out a broker to help them understand the coverage they need and how to complete the application, so brokers wouldn't be threatened by the direct solution for the business they did want to focus on.

In fact, the direct Quote and Bind offering is creating a benefit for the broker business because SCIF is taking what their mindset shift in underwriting has allowed them to do in terms of simplifying the application process, and is extending it to the broker channel with a simpler new business process there, too. They went so far as to take what they had learned about making the process better, and changed some of the decisions being made on a new policy administration system SCIF was developing at the time to make the entire business more efficient.

Coming back to their staff, I asked if the people who worked in the direct business before would feel threatened by the idea of a computer taking their jobs. In fact, the opposite happened.

Because the business was not thriving before, there wasn't a strong sense that you were working on something stable or that had opportunity. Now, because it is growing, the staff supporting direct-sold business see the Quote and Bind system as a purposeful commitment to the direct space, and created a real sense of pride in being on the direct team.

"Do you have the unified support of your Executive Committee? If you do, and they're committed, you're going to get a lot done."

– Dante Robinson
EVP, SCIF

Beyond just being part of a thriving business unit, their sense of pride is also coming from belonging to a dedicated team whose purpose is to provide SCIF's direct customers a great experience. This is the culture they have instilled in the team that places the direct customer at the center of their decision-making process. Perhaps equally importantly, the team also sees that the company's words are matching their behavior. The cultural and engagement benefit in that trust is immeasurable.

Aside from creating a healthy growth engine for SCIF, the real benefit is in how it got them to look at extremely challenging questions around what is *truly* necessary to know before you put out a price or go on risk. It helped them think about what to do if a prospect lies or if they do not really understand their business and its risk well enough to answer the questions accurately. Forcing Underwriting to get uncomfortable with the conventions it had relied on for over 100 years created an ability to SCIF to ensure it can evolve how it thinks about risk going forward.

Robinson left me with a really powerful bit of advice that he thinks is a foundational key to SCIF's success here. "Do you have the unified support of your entire Executive Committee? If you do, and they're committed to this, you're going to get a lot done."

Foundations for The Future

- Making innovation a top-down and bottom-up endeavor keeps you in touch with a constant and balanced flow of change and direction you may miss by doing one or the other.

- Engaging the entire organization openly, honestly and inclusively is important, but doing nothing with that engagement is almost the same as never engaging in the first place; ensure your innovative efforts lead to meaningful implementations of change so your culture genuinely moves.

- Be mindful of "we can't" or "we've never" mindsets rooted in history rather than evidence; be willing to challenge your people, and challenge them again to look at the problem multiple ways.

- Having true support and commitment from the executive team is central to making real, lasting change that capture the opportunities in front of you.

7. Ohio Mutual & Texting

When we think about how long many carriers have stood by their customers, we find a number of examples of carriers who have been committed to supporting people for over 100 years.

Ohio Mutual Insurance Group (Ohio Mutual or OMIG) is one such carrier, with its first policies issued in 1901 under the name "Ohio Mutual Tornado, Cyclone and Windstorm Association". Today, the carrier, still a mutual, remains based in Bucyrus, Ohio, in the heart of the Midwestern farm country it has been a part of for nearly 120 years. With over a quarter-billion in premium, it has expanded coverage to several other states, including through an acquisition in New England, and offers personal, commercial and farm coverage.

With such a rich and committed heritage, Ohio Mutual could have easily just kept doing what they've done well for so long, serve customers through dedicated staff who care about their work. And why change?

Working this way has earned OMIG a spot in the Wards fifty list of top-performing carriers six out of the last ten years. It has also come with great business success, both in terms of underwriting results and growth of over-10% in recent years in an industry that is arguably stagnant in real dollar terms.

The reason OMIG is not content to just keep doing what they've been doing is simple: they realized that what got them here won't get them where they need to go next as the world changes. They are aligned with this realization throughout the organization, from the associates through to the CEO and board.

On top of many of the headwinds we have discussed before, Ohio Mutual also has some others based on being a mutual carrier, which can limit access to capital since they cannot issue stock to finance major expansions or investments, such as their acquisition of Maine-based Casco Indemnity in 2010.

Many mutual carriers I've worked with have found themselves in situations where they feel they have fallen too far behind the market as a result of a different mindset around investment because of their different set of capital tools. On the flip side, mutuals also have an ability to act with a more long-term focus than stock companies might, because they do not have to worry about reporting to the stock market quarterly, a constant pressure to drive up share prices or dividends, and less of a continuous flow of commentary from analysts critiquing their activities.

Being significantly smaller than many of the carriers they compete against, including a hub of billion-dollar-plus carriers just a short drive away in Columbus, OMIG also has more limited resources and scale to push into innovations than larger competitors might.

Investing in some technology with a high initial cost can be hard when you don't have thousands of employees using the tool to spread that cost over to make it a palatable investment. For example, spending $10 million on a system to make sixty underwriters more efficient is harder to justify than spending $100 million for 800 or 1,000 underwriters. It also means OMIG would not qualify for the level of volume pricing discounts that typically come with higher license counts, further impacting their unit economics.

Conversely, Ohio Mutual is also too large to get by without investing in such tools or using workarounds to operate in a way a $50 million carrier might be able to. So, in a sense, they could be seen to be stuck in the middle, being too small to innovate cost-effectively, and too large to forgo innovating meaningfully.

One advantage they *do* have is that the level of hierarchy and corporate bloat they face is very low with a staff of just-over-230 people, mostly co-located in their Bucyrus headquarters or their New England regional office. This allows for potentially faster decision making, action, and an ability to involve a higher percentage of the staff in evolving how they work than larger companies might be able to do without concerted effort to do so. It also makes it easier to ensure everyone is on the same page culturally when it comes to moving forward.

That is to say, OMIG faced explicit challenges and had potential benefits from its size and structure that required using these advantages and navigating these challenges effectively to be able to succeed. There are many carriers in similar situations throughout the market.

With that background, CEO Mark Russell joined as President in September 2015, and saw the benefits OMIG had at its disposal. He took over from CEO Jim Kennedy, who was retiring and had done a fantastic job strengthening the company and putting in place a set of guiding principles.

Russell remembers the board quizzing him on the principles heavily when vetting him for the job because of how central they were to OMIG's success and culture. When he joined the company after being selected for the job, he led an effort not to change them, but rather to clarify them while keeping all the tenets in place.

He also recognized the threats and challenges the company was facing, both those described above, and those from a changing marketplace. In respect of these challenges, Russell decided two more guiding principles would be needed going forward – continuous improvement and earning loyalty.

For continuous improvement, the focus was on removing anything that created waste and gets in the way of delivering an exceptional customer experience. He wanted to really ground the company in the customer experience, and saw this as a five-year journey.

For loyalty, Russell felt strongly that, as a mutual, they must be here for their policyholders, and earn the right to renew each customer's business, rather than taking it as a given. And the same was true of their agents, where Ohio Mutual needed to earn the loyalty of each agent to represent the value and benefit of being insured by OMIG on each opportunity that came up.

One of his first strategic moves was to make a meaningful step forward on creating a culture of innovation to deliver on driving continuous improvement. He took one of the company's rising leaders, Bethany Foy, out of her day job, and gave her full-time responsibility for continuous improvement through innovation.

As I've discussed before, some companies do this without giving that person any resources or support. Russell did not give Foy any full-time staff, so you may think she was destined for the same fate. Instead, she was able to assemble a team of facilitators called "champions" from across every functional area who stayed in their day jobs, connected to the business and their functional area's needs, but with an explicit responsibility to help the company innovate.

This was a key structural design Russell made that paid dividends.

In creating innovation functions, many carriers set them up as standalone units that scour the market for new ideas and solutions, and bring them back into the company to find a home. Many are successful with this approach, but I have also seen several carriers where the functional areas have too much on their plate to consider what the innovation team has found, do not see the value in it, fail to see it as something that fits into the way their function works, etc.

As a result, the innovation team is not able to help the company innovate as effectively as intended, and the idea of innovation does not become a broad part of the culture, as Russell wanted to happen at OMIG.

By having people who still lived in their functions also be part of the team, Foy's Continuous Improvement group was consistently getting feedback from the functional areas across the organization about what they were dealing with, what they were interested in, and where they were hoping to move forward. And by having a cross-functional team, different functions could give ideas to or get insights from their peers in other parts of the business. For example, the Billing team may be facing an issue the Service team had been working to resolve and could share guidance with Billing on how to address it or a solution they were trying.

Of course, this could mean that OMIG would miss some of the industry trends and outside-in innovative thinking that a standalone function might bring, so Russell also engaged a consultant to scan the market regularly and bring ideas into the company on a quarterly basis.

This two-pronged strategy has resulted in a well-rounded approach to innovation at OMIG that engages the entire organization without missing external trends.

At the same time, Russell had setup a Customer Satisfaction team with a similar approach to the Continuous Improvement team, but instead it was about making the customer experience even better across the organization to drive loyalty. This was such an important issue in and of itself that Russell felt it needed dedicated focus from a standalone team, and named Chris Neeson from the Sales organization to head it.

Neeson and his team were tasked with finding a tool to measure and track customer and agent sentiment about Ohio Mutual, and put in place a survey mechanism to start measuring and reporting on Net Promoter Score (NPS), which started off right around the industry average in 2016, but has since increased by over 40% for customers and more-than-tripled for agents. Furthering the way agents value OMIG, Russell then added a third team under Vicki Edgington, purely focused on agent ease of doing business with OMIG.

The Claims team, like all other functions in the company, needed to be represented in both of the original groups Russell established. For Continuous Improvement, Auto Material Damage manager Kim Dallas joined to represent Claims. For the Customer Experience team, AMD and Subrogation Leader Andrea Presler joined that team.

For Dallas and Presler, there were some definite areas within each of their respective teams that overlapped as they thought about what Claims was most in need of, so the two of them worked closely on a number of items. One issue rose to the surface quickly for both of them, better communication solutions.

What they found was that claim reps were on the phone 70-80% of the day. While this meant they were directly working with insureds or working on insureds' claims diligently, it also meant they were very hard to get a hold of by customers, and they were struggling to find the space to make outbound calls to get claims moving or keep insureds updated on new developments and claim status changes.

On top of this, the world of communication has changed.

In many areas of our lives, we now communicate digitally and rapidly, through various messaging solutions. People do not rely on the phone like they used to, and many of us look at most telephone calls as likely coming from a telemarketer or spammer. Even if we would take a phone call, many of us simply are not available to do so during the day because of our jobs, and the claim person we need to talk to does not work in the evening when we are free. As a result, we end up playing phone tag, dragging out the claim process and frustrating everyone.

The phone is not a viable answer to solving the communication problem.

The insurance industry has relied heavily on faxing over the years, and is still an industry where faxing can be common, but it is neither customer-friendly, nor does it help with the move to paperless offices with digital records that we all desire. The number of carriers I've talked to who wish they could get rid of their fax machine is extremely high, and customers certainly do not want to fax, nor do most of them have access to fax machines, so faxing is not a viable answer, either.

We embraced email many years ago, which helped, but email today is not the fastest way to get a response from customers, and our inboxes are more inundated with spam than our phone lines are.

When I ran Claims for Hiscox, I found that customers would likely reply to my team at-best after a day, but more likely two-to-three days after we had reached out for information. And when insureds did respond, it often was not quite what we needed, so we would have to write them back, and wait another couple of days, hoping they would provide what was needed to move their claim forward. A simple question we needed to ask the insured therefore added three or four days to a claim's lifecycle. Email, though promising and helpful, was not proving to be a viable solution to the communication problem, either.

Something else was needed, and Dallas and Presler kept hearing from customers exactly what that was – *texting*. When claim handlers would get stuck in the communication game of missed calls and unanswered emails with customers, they would often hear from insureds something to the effect of, "Can't I just text you?"

Unfortunately, the reps never had a tool that let them say, "Yes, of course. I'd be happy to do that."

So OMIG tried something. Being a smaller carrier, they decided they could share a couple of mobile phones across the team in the late 2000s. This would allow them to receive texted-in photos from insureds. They had one person handle the mobile phone (a BlackBerry, at the time), and send the images to the adjuster who owned the claim the photos were related to. While this solved the problem of how to answer customers who wanted to send a text, it created all sorts of other issues.

For example, while they asked customers to include their claim number when sending the picture, some would forget or did not know their claim number, so you would hear people calling out on the floor things like, "I got pictures of a white F-150. Does that belong to anyone's claim?"

With a small team that was not receiving many texts, this was manageable, but obviously not scalable or ideal at all. Aside from it not being ideal for the Claims team, it was not great for customers overall. Imagine you are on the phone with an OMIG claim rep talking about your loss when you hear people shouting about unknown photos of damaged cars in the background. You can imagine that this may not create a sense of comfort around how your own claim might be handled.

Another issue that many carriers face is that adjusters started to just give in and offer their personal mobile phone number to customers. While this works well in the moment, it also means the customer now has the adjuster's personal phone number, and they invariably will start to call and text after hours, on weekends and nights, interrupting adjusters' personal lives. This also brings up another critical issue – evidencing.

In insurance, you need to ensure your risk or claim record is complete, with any relevant communications properly contained in that record. When customers start texting you on a cell phone, whether your own or one your employer provides, how do you get those texts into the claim file?

I know one carrier who did a pilot in a field office where they gave each adjuster a company-provided mobile phone, so they could text with customers. They had the adjusters block two hours each Friday to take screen shots of the texts to upload into the relevant claim files. While that is not ideal, the alternative (not properly documenting the files) is equally unattractive. If you do not have a complete claim file and there are any legal or regulatory actions on the claim (for example, coverage litigation or a DOI market conduct exam or audit), that adjuster's device would now become admissible in court, potentially exposing all of their texts, voicemails, emails and more to opposing counsel or the regulator rather than just those pertinent to the case at issue.

Discoverability is a real concern here, and something people in other industries may not understand. Solving for that through hours of tedious screen shot capturing and uploading is not a viable solution, either. If this one carrier's pilot is any indication, that means they expected 5% of their adjusters' work week would go to this activity. Aside from how the adjusters would feel about doing it (and how those feelings would likely lead them to stop doing it), this easily becomes a multi-hundred-thousand-dollar annual cost for even a small carrier.

In 2015, before the continuous improvement efforts had begun, the team at OMIG tried another solution. Most mobile operators, like Verizon and AT&T, let you use email to send a text to a mobile number using some combination of their ten-digit number and a special domain name the operator put in place for this purpose (for example, 1234567890@text.att.net or 1234567890@vtext.com).

The problem is, you needed to ask the insured who their mobile provider was, and they did not always know the answer, so that was difficult. Also, because you would be mixing email and text, you would run into issues with how the content was broken up for the customer because of the character and formatting limitations of texting that email does not adhere to.

Another constraint the OMIG team became aware of was needing to be compliant with a regulation from the telecom industry called the Telephone Consumer Protection Act of 1991, or TCPA.[13]

In the texting context, TPCA requires that you have consent from the customer to send them a text, and that you allow them to opt-out. Violations of TCPA carry a $1,500 penalty *per text*. Interpretation of the law and what constitutes a violation can be a gray area in the eyes of some, but I saw a claim for violation of TCPA from a single hour of unwanted marketing texts about a concert that resulted in $2 million in fines.

For an insurer, while they would not relish fines of that size, the bigger concern is that insurance regulators would then have cause to investigate the carrier's practices, putting their licenses in jeopardy. In other words, well-intentioned but poorly structured solutions for texting customers could result in a carrier being unable to write business in a state. That is not something insurers would want to risk, obviously.

Russell's push to create a culture of innovation in the company really struck a nerve in Claims given their struggle to make things easier for customers and themselves through texting in the past. The Claims function at Ohio Mutual had always done well over time, and therefore never got major investment because they were doing the job.

In 2017, Russell hired John DeLucia to run Claims, who worked with Kim Dallas and Andrea Presler in seeing that, if there is something they can do that makes the customer's experience markedly better and makes things easier or faster for their staff without significantly changing the cost structure, they should do it.

Texting was a space they could do something as it seemed to fit this

---

[13] See this Wikipedia entry on TCPA for more details:
https://en.wikipedia.org/wiki/Telehone_Consumer_Protection_Act_of_1991

concept, but they needed a better solution than they had found before. Even though their past attempts had not worked out as well as they had hoped, this was still an area where they could help customers, help their staff and do so without materially impacting their costs.

With that in mind, the team was connected with a company that created a new texting solution that OMIG had never explored before. They decided to do a pilot implementation to see if it would work for their needs. Specifically, it allowed OMIG's claim handlers to push a question out to a customer via text, and get a response back quickly. This sounded great and like it would have immediate value for the Claims team.

OMIG put together a team of pilot users to try the solution in early 2018. They quickly found how useful it was to get simple questions answered quickly. However, they also just-as-quickly found a few limitations to the solution, brought to light by frustrated pilot users.

Customers were used to texting being a conversation that spans time rather than a one-off moment to answer a specific question and then wait to possibly be asked another. Therefore, they would send additional texts at random times when they had their own question or had an update they wanted to share. And because there was no outgoing question they were responding to, these customer texts did not get to the adjusters.

You can imagine how customers felt when they heard nothing back from their adjuster, did not get answers to their own questions when they had been responsive to Ohio Mutual's, or when they thought something would happen on their claim as a result of their text, but never did because no one at OMIG knew the customer expected anything.

Keep in mind, in claim situations, some of those expectations could be quite important or serious, so doing nothing about them can be extremely consequential for the carrier and their customer. Adding to that, the usability for the OMIG staff was not good, even after the pilot team had some time to get used to the solution and how it worked, ensuring it was not a question of change management or adapting to something new. OMIG ended the pilot, choosing not to move forward with the solution, marking the third attempt to text with customers that was not really going to meet the need.

While some may see this as a failure or a sign that perhaps OMIG just isn't meant to text with customers, DeLucia, Presler, Dallas and the others involved at Ohio Mutual felt otherwise. They learned a great deal from this and their other experiences. They knew many reasons why texting can be complicated, and therefore knew what to look for in a solution. They brought their needs to the Continuous Improvement team and to their outside consultant, who had a few companies they were told to look at, and they did.

One company, Hi Marley, came to them through a referral from another partner they work with. Ohio Mutual reached out through Hi Marley's website to setup a demo call. I was working at Hi Marley at the time and was responsible for Sales, so I remember when OMIG's Claims Operations Leader, Kate Dodson, who works with Andrea and Kim, reached out. I was not able to join the initial demo call, but I heard the debrief about the quantity and quality of questions they asked, which made it clear that they knew a lot about two-way texting with customers already. That was rare in early-2019 as most carriers still were not looking at this space.

From the OMIG side, they noted how they peppered Hi Marley with a lot of questions, and consistently got responses that spoke directly to their greatest concerns. In calls with competitors, they felt they were either not being understood, getting the run-around, or told how they did not need to worry about that issue.

> "A big part of our decision was that the team at Hi Marley understands claims and the insurance business, whereas others just didn't get it."
>
> – Andrea Presler
> Leader, AMD & Subrogation,
> Ohio Mutual Insurance Group

Having transcripts of the texting conversations is one thing Hi Marley has had since the start, and was a major factor in my own decision to work with Hi Marley in my claims operation. It was how we would ensure that we had a complete claim file with all communication for regulatory and legal reasons.

Hi Marley's main competitor told Ohio Mutual, "Oh, you don't need transcripts. We'll just send you one if you really need it. Just ask us."

If you handle thousands of claims each year, month, week or day, as some carriers do, that is not a workable solution. The same goes for TCPA compliance.

Hi Marley was the only provider with the TCPA opt-in and opt-out process built into their solution, and the customer's responses during that process were made part of the transcript so carriers had evidence of their compliance.

That same competitor's response when questioned by OMIG about TCPA was, "Oh, just ask the customer on the phone before you text them. That's fine." That provider, not being from or dedicated to the insurance industry, did not understand these crucial needs and thought being dismissive of them was a good enough response rather than solving for them.

This was the first major driver of why OMIG ultimately chose Hi Marley, the pure-play focus on insurance. Andrea Presler said, "A big part of our decision was that the team at Hi Marley understands claims and the insurance business, whereas others just didn't get it." That summed up why they were hitting roadblocks or failure points with past attempts at texting, or reasons why they were uncomfortable with alternative options.

After that first call, the OMIG team circled back with each other, and then decided they should take the next step toward doing a pilot with Hi Marley. They brought us into their offices in Bucyrus to meet with Dallas, Presler, Dodson, DeLucia, representatives from IT and other members of the Continuous Improvement team from different areas in the company that were looking at texting, as well. We did a live demo for them, and answered a number of questions the IT team had around integration.

While excellent questions that showed how clearly the IT team understood what they were looking at, their questions were not actually immediately relevant.

With many SaaS solutions like Hi Marley or like CNA's use of Shift, little-to-no IT effort may be needed to go live, or at least to pilot some solutions. Because Hi Marley's solution lives in the cloud and can be accessed anywhere, the only IT requirements we had were that our website is not blocked, and that staff using the tool have Google Chrome on their machines (or Citrix or another managed environment a carrier may have). This is a very different level of requirements to those of many solutions carriers may have evaluated in the past.

What OMIG's IT team was asking about was around the potential API touchpoints down the road to understand how Hi Marley would fit into the future state they were working on for Claims and other functions. These questions were not about IT being a roadblock today when integration is irrelevant, but rather about having IT present and engaged in the meetings early on. In this way, DeLucia and his team were ensuring they had a partner in IT for that day when they do want to integrate more.

This is an important balance. New tools allow for quick, easy deployment and expansion, and many can go on that way in perpetuity.

For my team at Hiscox, we had Hi Marley come in one morning to train the Claims team, and within two hours, we were using it in live claims in a stand-alone implementation. However, if you ultimately want to integrate a solution in some way, while APIs make it easy, there is still at least an understanding needed internally about how that might work.

DeLucia and his team were smart to bring IT into the discussion early to ensure they had a chance to opine, could include this potential solution in their plans, and were not left to react to it later, which is often the case, and does not lead to good business-IT interactions.

The same is true for bringing other functional areas into the discussion, just like with how the Continuous Improvement and Customer Experience teams were built. While Claims was ready to move forward, and had gotten to a point with rep availability and customer requests that they really needed to solve the texting problem, other teams were starting to think about it, and would benefit from exposure to what Claims was doing in case it fit their needs, too, or they might have something to add to the discussion.

"To me, it's all about alignment. If you get the culture in place, then you align the goals and incentives – all of us are incented by our policyholder NPS since, as a mutual, our focus is on our policyholders."

– Mark Russell President & CEO, Ohio Mutual Insurance

A balancing point here is something I have seen at a few carriers where the need to include other functions that are not ready to act can sometimes slow the entire workstream down to a crawl as the organization feels it needs a single solution that answers everyone's needs before it tries anything.

That is a great idea, but if many of these needs are as yet undefined, you need to ask whether another approach of moving ahead where possible while including those who are still thinking about what to do is warranted.

OMIG and others I have seen chose to let the early-movers move, but include their other functions in the discussion to try to limit risk and make sure no functionality doors were closed that they might need open later (for example, Hi Marley can be integrated with payment solutions so you can send claim settlements to customers electronically, but if they explicitly could not work with the provider the Finance team just signed up with, then that would be a problem for a carrier).

This idea of bringing people from across the organization together as a team is exactly what Mark Russell was aiming for. "To me, it's all about alignment. If you get the culture in place, and then you align the goals and incentives — all of us are incented by our policyholder NPS since, as a mutual, our focus is on our policyholders — all our goals are aligned across all associates." What I saw in that first in-person meeting with Ohio Mutual was exactly this — a shared alignment through to the core despite all the different immediate needs and interests of the people in the room.

Russell went on to say what happens if you do not have this alignment. "I've worked at companies that carve up goals by units, and then you don't get teamwork. You end up battling each other for project resources, people resources, creating internal competition. I want all our focus on competition to be against our peers and competitors versus on any internal competition."

As we packed up after the demo, Presler and Dodson asked us to send them a contract for a pilot, so they could start the Legal review as they felt good about moving forward at that point. While this is extremely fast for a sales cycle in insurance, the team at OMIG had done a lot of homework on Hi Marley so they could move fast, and, as discussed above, had been working on what they really needed in a texting solution for almost a decade. They were ready and clear on what they needed to move ahead.

Once contracting was done, OMIG began a multi-week pilot, and then had to decide which adjusters to involve. They could have used the adjusters who worked on the last texting solution since they were familiar with texting in the context of a claim.

However, two things lead them to make a different decision. First, spreading pilot engagement out across the team means more of your people are part of the innovation and change movement, helping speak to Russell's initial goal around innovation. Second, many of those reps from the first pilot had a bad taste in their mouth from the experience, and were hesitant or gun shy about doing it again. Instead, the team chose seven different adjusters plus their mangers from the AMD team, and kicked off the pilot in September of 2019.

We came back on site, and showed the team that would be using Hi Marley for the pilot how the system works, walking them through a claim from FNOL to closure. What they quickly found, contrary to the last texting solution, was that it worked like other messaging solutions they were used to in their daily lives. It felt comfortable, and they seemed to get it even before we finished the first walk-through. We had booked a few hours for training, and DeLucia had graciously brought in an amazing breakfast spread that had barely been touched, but the team wanted to start using it, and we ended the training early.

We walked the floor while reps got into the system, answered a few questions here or there, and started to see heads popping up from above monitors and cubicle walls to share that they had a customer they were texting. We had planned to stay until late-afternoon, but by 2 p.m. it was clear that Ohio Mutual's team knew what to do, and did not need any hand holding.

While we got a few support requests over the first few days as people hit situations they had not faced before, things were quiet. We had expected each claim handler might have three or four new claims they put in the system in the first week, giving us around twenty-five cases to go through and hear feedback on. The team had put nearly three times that volume through the system as they started trying to text customers with existing claims who had been unresponsive, or where they were playing phone tag and getting nowhere. By the end of week two, we had seen over 100 claims go through Hi Marley, and Ohio Mutual started to get meaningful customer satisfaction data back from insureds.

While OMIG has been running a customer satisfaction survey program in Claims, this was different, and initially, something they were hesitant about. The Hi Marley survey is a simple question of how you would rate your claim experience and why you gave the score you did. It is not unlike what you do at the end of an Uber or Lyft ride. At the end of texting on a claim, when the case is being closed, a simple question is sent to the customer, asking them to rate their experience with Ohio Mutual on a scale of one (awful) to five (excellent).

OMIG did not want to over-survey their customers, a concern a lot of carriers gave us. We would generally ask that they keep the surveys in Hi Marley going during the pilot so they can see how customers feel about the solution, which they agreed to as a way to evaluate the pilot. They told us they expected to stop the surveys after that, as most who agree to use surveys in the pilot would warn us that they would do, too. Despite that, most end up with an experience like OMIG had, and choose to keep doing it, just like OMIG did.

Hi Marley had seen some outstanding customer satisfaction over thousands of cases, averaging 4.6 to 4.7. If you look at various customer rating websites, insurers generally score somewhere in the mid-2s to mid-3s. After you give your numerical rating, Marley, the persona who texts with you along with the adjuster, asks why you gave that score. Not only did Ohio Mutual get almost exclusively five-out-of-five ratings, but they were consistently getting feedback as to why customers were happy, or where they had wanted better service. That feedback proved invaluable to OMIG, who was not getting as much of this kind of detail behind the scores people were giving in other survey instruments. Over the life of the pilot, Ohio Mutual's average score was 4.9 out of 5, with 93% of customers giving their adjuster a five.

One concern people may have with texting is that it loses the human touch. Simple, quick, digital interactions lack the chance to show empathy that you might be able to give on a longer phone call. What Ohio Mutual found is that Hi Marley allowed them to show empathy in a different way. While their word choice was kind, supportive and clear, they found that being responsive shows empathy in and of itself.

"Exceeded my expectations. The ease of filing the claim and the quickness for a resolution is fantastic"

– Ohio Mutual Customer via Hi Marley

Hi Marley allowed them to track the speed of their responses, and OMIG's team was making first contact to customers who had asked to text within fifteen minutes of that request 79% of the time. And that includes nights and weekends since the timer is a twenty-four-hour clock, making this stat even more impressive.

They also found that giving customers relevant and helpful information before having to be asked for it is a way to show empathy by preemptively taking care of a customer's needs. With this tool, adjusters found themselves giving proactive updates on claims far more than before because it was so easy to do, and because they had time to do it since they were not stuck on the phone so much of their day.

The idea that you can show empathy, even when texting, came out in the comments from customers, including one of my favorites from Ohio Mutual's pilot. A customer named her claim handler specifically in giving thanks, which is a common occurrence in these responses. She said, "[Claim Rep] was very kind and helped me through a difficult time (getting a new vehicle), and processed the claim swiftly." Others called out the speed of communication and resolution. In cases where there was an issue, Ohio Mutual could actually get detail on what was not right, and could act on it, if appropriate. Of course, you may get people who give a bad rating because they wanted something they were not entitled to, or were perhaps exaggerating their claim (or "soft fraud," as discussed in the CNA case). The vast majority, however, were satisfied customers, and the feedback, positive and negative, has been a major benefit to Ohio Mutual, and one they are intent on keeping.

Between these strong customer experience results, a pilot team who loved the tool, and not seeing any of the pain points they had experienced with past efforts, the team at OMIG decided just two weeks into the pilot that they wanted to go forward with a full deployment across the rest of the Claims team.

Yet, while the team has generally adopted the tool, there have been some pockets of resistance. For some, it was perhaps being gun-shy as a result of past attempts at texting that were painful. For others, it is simply a question of changing how they have worked for years, and that can take time and perhaps retraining.

Ohio Mutual has used reports in Hi Marley to see who is a lower-volume user (or not using it in a given time period) to sit down one-on-one with that staff member to understand why they might not be using it, and try to work through that with them.

One thing that has been particularly helpful is using real data on the benefits of texting with customers to help people who might be hesitant to change. No one on the team wants to get bogged down with phone calls and voicemail tag. Looking at call records, adjusting for claim volume so it is a true apples-to-apples comparison, OMIG found that those really using Hi Marley on average handle roughly 250 calls per month. For those who have not been texting with customers, the average is around 350 calls per month. That difference works out to about five fewer calls each day. If we assume an industry-standard average call length of six minutes,[14] that means team members using Hi Marley gained back half an hour each day, or a savings of 10 hours per month on the phone. That works out to getting 6.7% of their time back to engage in helping customers and bringing their claims to resolution.

This becomes a very attractive carrot for people who are frustrated with the drudgery they have to go through to try to help people after a loss. I always said, "None of us signed up to play phone tag and make no progress when we decided to work in Claims. Yet that is what we end up doing instead of helping people put their lives back together when they need us most."

Hi Marley's experience with other carriers suggests a reduction of four calls per claim thanks to the tool. Ohio Mutual does not have an analogous per-claim stats in their metrics, but it is clear that they have seen a material benefit from Hi Marley on call volume.

From a bottom-line standpoint, Hi Marley has been able to test the impact on speed to claim closure and average loss cost, and seen 22% and 4%-or-better impacts on those measures, respectively.

You can imagine why that is when you think about how a claim proceeds. If you cannot connect with the insured, the repairs to their car can drag out longer, meaning you are paying for more days of a rental car or paying a body shop a storage fee while you try to work with the insured to pick up their car. Or in a Homeowners' claim, you may be paying for alternative housing for more nights than necessary because of communication-based delays in getting the home repaired and inhabitable again after a loss.

It is still early for Ohio Mutual, but they have now put thousands of claims through Hi Marley, so the potential for meaningful savings is starting to build up.

While the specific reason for using Hi Marley – to be able to text with customers during claims – is being met, Ohio Mutual has used it to catalyze other innovative thoughts in Claims (like changes to their FNOL process), and other areas where they are thinking about

---

[14] "9 Important Call Center Industry Standards and How to Beat Them," Astute Solutions, June 27, 2019.

communicating differently.

That is perhaps one of the biggest lessons from this example. Through years of trying different things, OMIG stayed open and insisted on learning each time. They sought advice, both internally and externally, engaged with their people, and stayed open to solving a true customer need rather than getting discouraged by setbacks or walk away because of perceived failures that were really just bringing them even greater clarity on what they needed to do.

Foundations for The Future

- Successful innovation efforts pair cross-functional, bottom-up demand for new ideas with outside-in sourcing of solutions that would be missed otherwise.

- Ensuring company-wide alignment on shared values and goals helps teams work together to serve policyholders and beat the competition rather than focus on competing with each other for resources.

- Keeping a guiding idea, like OMIG's thought that making the customer experience better while improving things for employees without materially hurting their cost structure was a good target to aim for when considering innovative ideas. Making it more complicated will likely lead to dismissing ideas that may be worth trying.

- Repeated, failed attempts at solving a problem can lead to quitting and negativity. Instead, look at them as opportunities to really hone in on what you need to be successful when deciding if a solution has the ability to stick long-term.

8. EMPLOYERS & API-Enabled Distribution

Over 106 years ago, what is now the publicly traded, national, Workers' Compensation carrier EMPLOYERS, was formed by the State of Nevada as a state-funded, monopolistic, monoline WC insurer.

If you employed people in Nevada, you had no choice but to use the state fund for coverage. This is different from what we saw with SCIF, which was a market-of-last-resort in California. After new legislation that was approved in 1995, the state WC market was opened up to competition from private carriers in 1999, ending the state fund's monopoly and forcing it to compete with the 250 carriers who started writing the day the law was enacted in 1999.

At the same time, the state legislature voted to privatize the fund, turning EMPLOYERS into a mutual carrier owned by its Nevada policyholders. As CEO Doug Dirks shares on an EMPLOYERS podcast,[15] the reason why was that the fund had a $2.2 billion deficit, and was losing $1 million per day. With this cash burn, they had an eighteen-month runway before they could no longer pay the 50,000-plus injured workers they were meant to be there to help. Aside from the risk to those injured workers who depended on their WC coverage to help them through the tough time they faced post-injury, EMPLOYERS' deficit was twice the state's annual operating budget,

---

[15] Varahachaikol, Adam, Interview with Doug Dirks, President & CEO of Employers Holdings, Inc., "The EMPLOYERS Emphasis, Episode 1," podcast audio, October 21, 2019.

putting the solvency of the State of Nevada at risk, as well.

Today, EMPLOYERS writes business in all but the four monopolistic states. Now a public-company since their NYSE listing in 2007, they operate with five underwriting companies including their direct, digital carrier Cerity, in addition to their broker-distributed business. The group ended 2019 with nearly $700 million in premium and over 100,000 policyholders (versus 6,600 when they went public). Most importantly, the company's financial position is markedly different today, with strong reserves and investments and an A- (Excellent) rating from AM Best.

While the stability and size of the company have changed, perhaps more profound is how the business changed in the way it thinks and operates. CEO Doug Dirks has been with EMPLOYERS for over a quarter of a century, and recalls having to bring his own PC when he joined the company in 1993, when it was still a monopolistic state fund and only had traditional green screen terminals. Documents were going out to insureds and others after being individually typed and mailed until a document generation solution was implemented in 1998, barely over twenty years ago.

Needless to say, change has accelerated since then, but it is important to understand how recently EMPLOYERS was still dramatically behind the curve operationally to set the stage to appreciate where the story will be going.

Things really started to pick up with what Dirks and COO Steve Festa set in motion from 2014 through 2017 as several new executives joined the company, including a new Chief Underwriting Officer (Larry Rogers), Chief Information Officer (Jeff Shaw), Chief Data Analytics Officer (Tom Warden), Chief Claims Officer (Barry Vogt), SVP of Business Transformation & Operational Excellence (Aaron Mikulsky) and Chief Sales & Marketing Officer (Ray Wise).

The vision Dirks and Festa had articulated that attracted all of these leaders was around cultural and operational values needed to transform the business even further from where it had been not twenty years prior when it was still part of the state. They focused on breaking down bureaucracy and breaking down the silos that exist between functions at many carriers.

Having worked at a former state fund myself, I know the ingrained nature of such bureaucracy due to being a *literal* bureaucracy with *literal* politics (not just a word to describe a difficult corporate culture) can be incredibly hard to shake.

With true commitment from the top, EMPLOYERS stood a good chance. But this commitment was not just coming from the CEO, it was coming from a CEO who had been a veteran of the organization, which is not always a common source of culture change. This is a good reminder that any organization can change from within, regardless of whether the person leading that change is an insider or not, and regardless of how deeply-ingrained the old culture may be.

Dirks appealed to the rest of the executive team on the shared frustration everyone has had in their careers around how difficult it can be to get things done in many organizations. Regardless of your position, no one ever enjoys or wishes for that to be the way it is. He asked a simple question of how they as an organization can operate *together* across Distribution, Pricing, Claims, Finance, Service, IT, HR, etc. It was a movement from having an idea and feeling like you should keep it for yourself to one of how you can share it and collaborate across the organization.

With the leadership of the company aligned in the desire to achieve more things with greater ease and collaboration, there was a unanimous alignment right at the top. Next, Dirks ensured the rest of the organization was aligned, too.

Each leader spread the thinking to their organization, but Dirks also communicated openly and transparently about the direction and thinking with everyone in the organization. Rather than seeing EMPLOYERS as a set of regional businesses or departments, he wanted people thinking nationally and enterprise-wide. That means not just doing things to help your immediate area, but thinking about how you can contribute to the organization as a whole.

This started to create an ability to row together and move the whole ship forward by seeing the value of the collaborative whole rather than focusing on what any one oar can do in its own oarlock. People started to feel comfortable bringing ideas to leadership, and saw that the best ideas would move forward regardless of their source.

This alignment was then pointed at what would be the right area of the market for EMPLOYERS to focus on – small businesses, which are the lifeblood of the economy since 89% of companies have fewer than fifty employees. The question was then how best to capture and serve the small business market.

The tip of that spear lies in leaping ahead on distribution to capture how small business insurance is bought and sold as it was evolving in front of EMPLOYERS' eyes. Small business is the only part of the Commercial P&C market that has moved to digital distribution, including direct writers, aggregators, digital agencies or brokers, online trading platforms and more. I saw this first hand at Hiscox, with our direct business.

Ray Wise points out that agents have responded to the shift in their insureds' habits by responding to their needs around the clock since small business owners' personal and work lives often intertwine, and mobile devices lead them to manage their business even at home at night or on the weekends. As Wise puts it, "Small business insurance is now being done at home in people's bunny slippers."

While the footwear may vary, there is no question that this is the case. If you want to play in this space, you have to meet insureds and distributors how, when and where they want you to, which takes offering solutions agents and brokers will need in the future as their worlds continue to change.

EMPLOYERS had already expanded to over thirty states by then (and now writes in all but the four monopolistic states of Washington, Ohio, Wyoming and North Dakota). This geographic expansion inherently solved some distribution-based constraints for EMPLOYERS as they became a more attractive option to brokers who were placing coverage for increasingly-geographically-diverse business customers which required focusing on carriers with broader footprints. It also can help smooth losses based on geography that a more concentrated carrier could not mitigate.

What geographic spread did not solve for on the quest to be a leader in the small commercial market was on the technological, data analytics and operational pieces of the puzzle. Dirks uses the Wayne Gretzky quote, that's already been featured elsewhere in this book, of skating to where the puck will be and in realizing being a fast-follower is not the answer. EMPLOYERS would have to be a leader in how it delivers its products and services to customers if it not only wants to thrive, but even just to survive given the shifts happening in the market.

The word "customer" here is one several carriers debate about. Who is the customer? Is it the insured? Is it a broker or agent? Is it the injured worker?

I have been involved in many deep discussions, debates and exercises to answer this question for many carriers, and EMPLOYERS took a decidedly different path here which really resonated with me. Each of these parties is a customer that needs to be served well. You cannot neglect or de-prioritize one and expect to succeed overall. For example, you can develop the best coverage, pricing and claims service available, but if your quote and bind processes are too painful, agents still will not give you their business.

To that end, COO Steve Festa created a new position of Chief Customer Experience Officer (CXO) in 2019 to pull together the company's focus on the idea of the customer.

Craig Borens, who had been with the company, leading various customer-facing efforts, was named EMPLOYERS' first CXO, putting additional emphasis on the idea of serving customers, however that term may be defined.

Ray Wise summed up the way they consider this question simply and brilliantly. He said:

"How can you deliver an agency an exceptional customer experience if you neglect the policyholder or injured worker? If there's an issue with the policyholder experience, who are they going to go to? You just made it harder on the agent by neglecting the policyholder or injured worker.

On the flip side, if you've delighted the policyholder, it makes it easier for the agent all around – in how their client values them, in keeping the insured happy, in having to re-market the account because you did not make them look good and in recommending you to the next insured looking for coverage."

While building new tools and processes is needed, how you build them is the difference between wasted investment and unlocking growth in distribution. It can be tempting to see new technology and ideas coming out and having an "if we build it, they will come" mentality. This is a bit of what we saw in the early 2000s with the various exchanges and e-commerce-enabled trading platforms that inevitably fizzled out. Instead, you have to focus on what the agents need, and make that the core of what you're doing and why, or you will end up spending significant money on things you do not need or cannot benefit from.

On Wise's team was Chris Champlin, Director of

Alternative/Digital Distribution, and a ten-year veteran of EMPLOYERS as Ray Wise joined.

Since early 2016, Champlin had been looking at the idea of APIs and how they could facilitate working with distribution partners whenever and however they wanted. Unfortunately, Champlin had not found success in getting his idea approved yet. With Ray Wise and new-CIO Jeff Shaw joining, that would change.

Shaw moved the IT organization to an Agile delivery approach from a Waterfall approach, as many carriers have done in the past few years. Agile is an iterative development approach based on requirements and solutions built by cross-functional teams. The focus is to develop and deliver software quickly and repeatedly, helping to keep what gets released aligned to what is needed as development is constantly being fed by requirements as they may shift over time. This contrasts with the traditional Waterfall approach of taking in a set of requirements, going off and building everything over a longer period of time, then delivering a complete solution that may no longer meet the business's needs as requirements shifted during the development period.

Changing to Agile allowed EMPLOYERS to listen to even small ideas as they had the flexibility in delivery to take on smaller projects that would not fit with the typical overhead of the Waterfall approach.

As Champlin put it, moving to Agile allowed them to solve for one or two problems instead of World peace. The API idea ended up being the first Agile project at EMPLOYERS, and was a perfect fit for the approach.

Champlin's vision tied to an imperative Wise shared, "Getting our transactions on the glass faster enables an agent in a seamless fashion to do business with their customers. We need to find ways to do that." APIs were a clear way to do this.

EMPLOYERS was already working with traditional agents, purely-digital agents, wholesalers, payroll solutions, franchise program administrators, technology vendors, and other carriers who do not have their own existing or robust-enough Workers' Comp offering. APIs would enable these distribution partners to publish to and consume from EMPLOYERS' systems. Specifically, APIs could be used in the quoting and binding process by letting a distribution partner capture information about a risk, pass it to EMPLOYERS for rating, and quickly receive coverage and price options to present to a prospect. If the prospect selects an option from EMPLOYERS, APIs could be used to bind coverage and transmit key information and necessary documents.

Much more could be done with APIs, but the initial idea needed to stay focused on facilitating the first step in the distribution equation of getting an EMPLOYERS quote in front of prospects quickly and easily for their partners. Making the project too big would mean it no longer fits into the Agile approach for quick turnaround.

The needs of distribution partners would clearly differ, as well, with many of them likely requesting custom solutions or having unique needs. Again, this could be a point of complication for delivery of a working API solution, so Champlin and the others on his team, which numbered just five in total with an underwriter, two developers and an IT business analyst, decided to stay focused on a small set of distribution partners.

> *"Getting our transactions on the glass faster enables an agent in a seamless fashion to do business with their customers. We need to find ways to do that."*
>
> – Ray Wise
> Chief Sales Officer,
> EMPLOYERS

This was a first for EMPLOYERS, both in building APIs and running an Agile project, which meant they had to lean heavily on input from their distribution partners to understand what was needed for this to succeed. That taught them a valuable lesson in how important it is to ask your customers what they need and what problems they are trying to solve for rather than presuming you know. Since the team was so small and new to this, they had no choice initially, but soon realized this need for customer input was a strength, not a weakness. While they wanted to deliver one API to one partner in the initial release, they worked with a group of five or six early-adopter partners to gather requirements for what they needed to do.

To ensure success given the tight resources and the desire to get to market while it was still largely-untapped, the team decided on a few philosophical guidelines:

1. Meet the customer (using the broad definition of customer that includes distribution partners and end-insureds) where they want to buy rather than forcing them to buy one way or another.

2. Make sure the product and approach are scalable, avoiding splintering into multiple, customized APIs by having one solution that is enhanced as new functionality needed across partners is identified.
3. Have the right business development resources who are not just sales resources, but also can be technical resources on how best to use the APIs so partners have a consistent, single, knowledgeable point of contact for how to work with EMPLOYERS and succeed.

We discussed the first idea above, which was really the impetus for the API project in the first place. The second guideline was quite interesting and very hard to stay true to as you face partners insisting on a special need they have that must be met.

What the team learned is that, often, when the partner is asking for something custom, you have to look past the immediate request and get into what they are trying to achieve. In understanding that, you can unearth a more universal solution that could bring value to other partners.

Champlin and the team took these unique requests to their partner group as a whole to test the value. If an idea was valued by the rest of the partners, it was worth building. If not, either more understanding was required, or they would pass on the idea. With limited resources, you cannot expect to respond to every custom request and still deliver overall, a lesson most insurtech startups face (but many do not learn) repeatedly as they want to please carriers they feel lucky to count as customers.

This notion of scalability also extended to how many new opportunities they would try to go live with at a given time. Starting with the first release in October of 2017 and the second partner going live by February of 2018, the team had built up the capability to release one new partner every thirty days with their team of five.

In addition to developing and testing the API to be able to go live, Champlin's Alternative/Digital Distribution business development function, which was just him at the time (and has grown since), would source and open new distribution partner opportunities or cultivate existing ones to bring into the API program.

They set an overall limit of no more than five partners in process at any given time to keep them from being overwhelmed and risk delivery. After nine months of delivery and getting their processes and tools really solidified, they removed that constraint. That is, they ensured they had built a scalable delivery approach, and then let it scale once they did so.

The business development guideline may seem irrelevant to an Agile IT project, but it was critical to EMPLOYERS' success here. They found it to be extremely important to have the relationship owner able to meet the partner's needs across the board. After all, despite all the talk about APIs, few were really using them yet in meaningful ways, and since digital distribution of Workers' Compensation insurance was new, as well, you had two unknowns partners were dealing with, so giving them a single expert who could help them across the board was valuable. Some of EMPLOYERS' distribution partners were even new to insurance and others were new to Agile (or did not use it yet), so "across the board" could become a very broad notion.

> "Some carriers try to push so much into their API, and it may be more than the partner is ready for. We saw how to be more attuned to what the agent wants. This helps us standout when those decisions come around on who to work with."
>
> – Chris Champlin
> Director of Alternative/
> Digital Distribution,
> EMPLOYERS

With these guidelines in place, the team delivered functionality in two-week sprints, and generally found things were going smoothly. Where they hit bumps in the road were generally when they were working with a partner who was new to Agile, not using it yet, or had a technology vendor they were working with to make changes to their own system to be able to connect to EMPLOYERS' API.

This meant the teams at EMPLOYERS and the partner could get out of sync, threatening to delay delivery. For example, EMPLOYERS might have something ready to test, but the partner's team was not ready to connect to the API yet. This required staying very close to partners to keep everyone aligned.

Champlin had a mindset he shared with the team to set the right perspective in these moments and support their partners. He called it being, "aggressively patient." He said, "We have to keep them moving, but have to be patient at the same time. They are not just doing Workers' Comp, and are not just working with EMPLOYERS. We cannot expect them to always make our need priority number one."

While some partners might have required keeping this mindset front and center more (though Champlin was clear that they were all great to work with and helped EMPLOYERS understand what their APIs needed to be like to be successful for all involved), several partners were in lock-step with EMPLOYERS. When partners also followed Agile, Champlin said they would follow a change or release from EMPLOYERS with the related change on their end within two or three days.

Contrary to what many outsiders perceive of insurance companies and certainly different from the picture of EMPLOYERS I gave earlier in this case, the team found that EMPLOYERS is generally ready to go live before their partners are. And they are faster than other carriers have been, based on what their distribution partners are telling them. Champlin thinks this is for a few reasons. First, because EMPLOYERS is focused on one line, that reduces complexity for EMPLOYERS and their partner in going to market. Second, staying true to the idea of solving one or two problems at a time, EMPLOYERS kept the scope tight and focused on their API while some carriers have tried to deliver a complete suite of APIs across the functional spectrum. That has obvious implications for how long development, testing and release will take, and areas where things can go wrong or not be good enough for the need. EMPLOYERS could stay laser focused on creating the best quoting and binding process through its APIs because that is all they were solving for, and just for WC.

In terms of adoption by the market, as they cross the three-year mark with the solution, EMPLOYERS will have over twenty-five distribution partners using their APIs. With such healthy adoption, the team has gotten a good sense of how their API strategy has worked out.

EMPLOYERS set two major areas they would look to when judging success: growth in the business and expense control. They set high bars to measure success for each of those areas, and have surpassed them. While they would not share specifics on the expense side, one thing they shared on the growth side was around submission flow.

The APIs now drive 40% of EMPLOYERS' submission activity today. If the APIs merely cannibalized other business, or if the whole number went down while the mix changed, this would not alone be a sign of success. Or you could say that more submissions in and of themselves are not valuable if they are not converting to bound policies, and you would be absolutely right. Increasing the front of the sales funnel while having hit rates deteriorate is not a recipe for success. However, since the APIs went live, EMPLOYERS has recorded record high numbers of not just submissions but also quotes *and* binds. And further proof that APIs are not cannibalizing their core business (outside of partners who have moved to the API), they have seen an increase in their traditional business on top of the growth through the API. Part of that comes from improvements to their core system to facilitate the APIs that are benefitting the non-API business, as well.

Beyond the immediate-term business success, going back to Dirks' desire to skate to where the puck is going, EMPLOYERS has still not seen much competition with other carriers working with their partners through APIs. This makes the work a clear win; it is delivering material business benefit while also putting them far ahead of many of their competitors.

And they continue to skate to where the puck is heading.

Champlin was quick to point out that, just because they are ahead of the pack and doing well with their API, they have and will continue to evolve and enrich it. What they released in 2017 is very different from what they have today. It has evolved significantly due to the quality of customer feedback and input from how the team at EMPLOYERS continues to engage with distribution partners on the idea.

This constant flow of feedback and ideas also means EMPLOYERS has a seat at the table as to where the industry is going and where innovation is happening. While giving them a chance to stay ahead of the curve, it also affords EMPLOYERS the chance to deepen their distribution relationships and help shape what the future looks like.

This extends to all the emerging ways distribution is happening. The API is good for any kind of distribution channel, so as new approaches arise or existing ones shift, EMPLOYERS has the tools, in the APIs and their approach to the market, to serve those changes in distribution. The way EMPLOYERS approached the solution allows them to continue to meet all the new and changing ways customers want to buy.

Foundations for The Future

- When trying to shift culture, appealing to shared visions of what a better world looks like can serve leaders, whether they come from outside the carrier or have been part of an organization for years.

- Focusing your efforts to address the most important questions facing you and your customers can speed go-to-market efforts and limit delays and major points-of-failure that are more easily avoided through controlled scope with specific aims.

- Recognizing the interplay of different types of customers rather than choosing one type over the other protects you from creating points of failure for one customer on your journey to create success with another, blocking your overall success from being possible.

- Getting regular, honest feedback from customers not only leads to building better solutions they actually value, but gains you an invaluable seat at the table as your customers think about what their future needs will be.

9. AXA XL & Innovating in Construction Insurance

Gary Kaplan is President of AXA XL's nearly-billion-dollar North American Construction business. It is a business unit focused purely on the construction vertical, providing nine different insurance products that construction firms need, like Workers' Compensation, Builders' Risk, Property and more.

As part of AXA XL, aside from many of the dynamics discussed when looking at other carriers in this book, Gary and his team have several additional ones, like being acquired by a Paris-based global insurance giant, which did not have a P&C foot print in North America, as well as the uncertainty about culture and power that can come with being acquired.

Not long before AXA acquired XL in September of 2018, XL themselves had acquired fellow specialist Catlin (in May of 2015), and had been going through their own post-merger integration since then. No matter how well any integration goes, there is always disruption, so Kaplan and his team went from one major change to the next, and went from being the acquirer to being acquired in fewer than three years. Not only that, but XL had faced the threat of not surviving the Global Financial Crisis of 2008 just a decade before.[16]

---

[16] Prior to May 2015, the company was known as "XL." From May 2015 to September 2018, the company was known as "XL Catlin." After September 2018, it has been known as "AXA XL," which is how I generally refer to it for simplicity and continuity despite what it was called at each point in the story.

During that particularly-tumultuous time for many companies, Kaplan had been with another carrier, which he spent twenty-one years at after starting his career as a risk engineer. While at his prior employer, Kaplan had been introduced to something that would change things for him in a profound way, and came to define his leadership style.

The concept, taught to him and others at the company by Schaffer Consulting, is called Rapid Results Initiatives[17] or RRI for short, and it closely mirrors what we now refer to as Design Thinking, which was discussed in the SCIF case.

It was an approach to implementing successful change through managing it as a short-term project. Using RRI, a leader would assemble a small team of six-to-twelve people, challenge them with an issue or share an opportunity with them, and let them do a bit of Blue Sky thinking on it. From the ideas they came up with, the group then narrows the list down to one or two to focus on, and then see what result they can achieve on those ideas over a ninety-day period.

Design Thinking is usually focused on a problem or question, and Kaplan was quick to point out how well RRI worked in looking at opportunities and developing paths to bringing them to fruition in addition to tackling questions or problems.

> "It's always a slow start when you introduce it, but then it takes off and people around the business and in management see the value."
>
> – Gary Kaplan
> President, Construction, AXA XL

What RRI is *not* is a once-and-done solution to getting everyone to embrace change (or the RRI approach itself). It takes time, iteration and a commitment to the approach for it to bed-in. Having been through that lifecycle at two carriers now, Kaplan is familiar with the need to keep at it while you build an army of believers throughout a business. He shared that sentiment when he said, "It's always a slow start when you introduce it, but then it takes off and people around the business and in management see the value."

He started to talk about it as an approach to leadership that he calls

---

[17] "Rapid Results: Carving complex initiatives into a series of fast-cycle efforts," Schaffer Consulting.

Project-Centric Leadership. Kaplan sees the job of a leader as being to figure out how to use a limited number of resources effectively to move the organization forward through a series of small projects. The projects come together in a portfolio that makes up the business's operational plan, which gives people the direction needed to stimulate profitable growth, drive productivity and empower each individual to have an impact.

When Kaplan joined what was then-XL in 2010, he brought this approach with him, and ensured that everyone in the Construction team participated in at least one RRI project per year in some capacity. With this much focus, the Construction business has been able to do fifty projects per year for the past decade. And these are not just projects for project's sake. They are real initiatives that collectively move the business forward while engaging everyone on the team in that mission.

In fact, the first RRI project at XL was to establish the Construction business itself as a focused vertical solution within XL. Since they had so few people on board in Kaplan's team, the first official RRI project at XL was done outside of his team. That project was done to help drive success with cross-selling activities across XL's North America businesses. Soon after that project's successful completion, another was done, and at that point, RRI became a regular part of XL.

Culturally, this is not a surprise in many ways. As a specialist carrier, XL has always been focused on meeting specific market needs that require technical expertise and deep knowledge to meet. And with many of their underwriters, claims professionals and others having direct experience in the areas they insure, XL's employees could more easily put themselves in the customer's mindset than might be possible at other carriers. Additionally, XL was early for an insurer in the creation of their own corporate venture capital (CVC) unit when they formed XL Innovate in 2015 to look for enabling technology that could change their own industry or those of their insureds.

With XL Innovate and other channels like cold-outreach on LinkedIn or via email bringing new ideas and technologies into the company, Kaplan and his team noticed a material increase in the number of new things coming their way in 2017. This was the perfect context to use the RRI approach to evaluate each of these ideas as opportunities through a small team over a fixed period of time. In this way, Kaplan's unit could see whether an idea had value, and actually piloted several ideas with customers to really test their viability.

In early 2017, one company came through to Kaplan via a connection at a large, global reinsurance broker. That solution, from a company that was called Weather Analytics at the time and today is called Athenium Analytics, used extremely advanced tools to predict weather with specificity and detail most people had never seen before or thought possible. It was an offshoot of work done for the US intelligence community, so you can imagine the level of power in the data and the tool, and the rigorous demands Athenium had to live up to when developing it around things like information security and accuracy. What surprised the team at AXA XL was how easy it was to interact with and get insights from.

While it was very interesting, Kaplan was left unsure if it was a technology in search of a need as he did not want to get into Weather insurance. Though he did not want to insure it directly, he did see how weather had great impact on his business and the business of his customers. Bad weather can delay construction projects materially, and at the scale of the projects many of AXA XL's customers operated, a day delay could mean hundreds of thousands of dollars lost, or more.[18] And a sudden gust of wind that had not been expected could bring down a crane, creating a sizable Property claim, while injuring workers or bystanders in the process, leading to Workers' Compensation and Liability claims on the scale of millions of dollars on top of a large Business Interruption claim. The team could see how this data could be incredibly powerful for them and for their insureds.

The team from Athenium took that reaction and feedback to heart. With no background in Construction when they came in the first time, Athenium endeavored to learn a great deal about the space to understand how their tools could empower AXA XL and its customers, and built a new application of their weather data and analysis suite specifically geared to the construction industry. Calling their solution GaugeConstruction, Athenium showed how the analytics they created could help protect a construction project from the impact of weather, and then how it could be used post-loss to adjust claims more accurately and timely.

---

[18] "Weather assessment solution: Helping control risks, time and Money", AXA XL, October 28, 2019.

Kaplan had an ideal candidate for an RRI project.

He gathered a team together, which quickly decided on three customers that would be good to do a pilot implementation with to see how viable and valuable the solution was. Today, when selecting customers to do a pilot with, the team is fairly prescriptive on how the tool should be used. Back then, they had not yet thought about that kind of structuring for the RRI, and let the customers decide what to do with the Athenium solution. This ended up giving AXA XL a much broader understanding of how GaugeConstruction could be leveraged and opened the door to learning things they would not have considered when setting the pilot up if they had been more prescriptive about usage.

The three customer pilots kicked off that summer, right after introducing the Athenium idea to AXA XL's Customer Council. Since the pilot customers did not have explicit guidance on what to do with the tools from Athenium, they each used the tools in different contexts and for different purposes within their business. One used it in the field to help manage live construction projects. One used it in their risk management function. The third used it purely for the data it produced, which they wanted to extract and use in various parts of their business.

The pilots ran as RRI projects themselves, which customers in the pilots really appreciated. They found the approach to be very different from past pilots they had done, mainly because of the fixed structure of the approach. Rather than going on for a long time or perhaps being open-ended, the ninety-day timeline gave a sense of intentionality to the pilot since you had a definitive, limited period to use, evaluate and give feedback on the solution before it was gone.

Justin Gress, who at the time led Strategic Operations for AXA XL Construction, shared how people often get on projects seemingly-forever, creating project burnout, a potential to lose interest in the project as it drags on, and room for there to be a lack of coordination because timescales are so long. With the RRI's ninety-day focused approach, people involved were more focused on the project given the somewhat-compressed timescale versus past experiences. The structure also had explicit periods to check-in, give feedback and adjust the approach, again, creating more direction and focus than they had seen in other pilots.

Gress described the benefits of the structure directly when he shared:

> "People get on projects, and they end up being on them forever. RRI is a way to time-box it in. And that's good with the customer, too, so they know what they're signing up for. There's a bit of a hustle for those ninety days, having everything built around that. Because everyone knows when we're going to be done, we can price the pilot around that fixed timing, and can put in the necessary check points.
>
> Giving the customer and our own internal people a feeling of what to expect is a big thing. The RRI concept has really helped us a great deal when we've gone to customers. They've heard us talk about it, they've heard other customers talk about doing it, and it's a way for them to experience and participate in innovation with us."

One of the pilot customers for GaugeConstruction, a New York-based, multi-billion-dollar, national contractor, immediately saw the value in the solution when learning of the idea and specifically the solution's prediction of wind at altitude. For construction firms like this one that employ a lot of cranes across their projects, this is invaluable information. Just two weeks before being asked to join the pilot, the contractor had a near-loss of a crane on a project due to wind, so their Risk Manager realized how Athenium's tools could have helped them avoid that situation (or, worse, an actual loss). It was not just theory to this customer, but something they clearly understood and valued right off the bat.

As a result, by Thanksgiving of 2017, AXA XL had gathered a wealth of real-world experience and feedback from these three customers. Athenium, who did not have any understanding of construction before getting involved with the AXA XL team, had built up a deep knowledge of it through their own research and the feedback from the pilot, which they took in very seriously.

After the pilot closed, Athenium went quiet for a few months while they digested everything and adjusted GaugeConstruction accordingly. When they came back to AXA XL in early 2018, they had dramatically evolved their solution to speak directly to the customer needs revealed in the pilot. They saw how the weather data would help on the insurance side, avoiding or in adjusting losses. But, as Gress put it, "it's really about helping the customer with bigger needs they have beyond insurance, and you uncover that through these RRI processes. If there are things we can do to help our customers run their business that go beyond insurance or risk, that goes a long way."

Athenium made some meaningful changes in the software to help go beyond insurance. They took the solution from a group of separate weather-related tools to an integrated suite, while adding and adjusting functionality and usability. They also had a breakthrough capability that allowed construction firms to accurately predict lost days when bidding on a project using science.

In the construction industry, when a contractor bids on a project, they need to estimate the number of workdays they will lose to weather-related work stoppages. As some major projects can go on for years, such as building a skyscraper or major public works project, your ability to accurately predict the impact of weather becomes more luck than anything else. Common tools used would be past experience and the Farmer's Almanac.

I remember when Hurricane Ike hit in September 2008, the corridor of damage left in its wake extended all the way up to Ohio. I doubt anyone predicting weather stoppages when bidding on projects in the Midwest had contemplated the impact of an Atlantic hurricane, and I doubt the Farmer's Almanac did, either. If your estimate had enough contingency in it for such unforeseen events, then you would be ok. But, according to data AXA XL compiled, if you are off by just a single day on a $200 million project, that could cost the construction firm a quarter of a million dollars.[19]

And, of course, every day of contingency you bake into your bid that a competitor does not include makes you that much more expensive and therefore less likely to win the bid. That makes accurately predicting the impact of weather on a project a major competitive advantage in winning business and factor in the financial success (or even survival) of a contractor.

Unlike the luck-based approach, Athenium brought deep science and analytics to the estimation of weather-related delays in construction. Now, firms could enter the details of the project they

[19] *Ibid.*

were bidding on, and the Athenium tools could give them a detailed estimation of lost days so they could build their bids accordingly. This came directly from the pilot experience with AXA XL's customers.

AXA XL's Construction team continued to work with Athenium on spreading GaugeConstruction, trying to drive adoption of the tools as much as possible as it only helps reduce loss and improve results if it is widely adopted. They connected Athenium with the Association of General Contractors (AGC), who had Athenium present at their national meeting with construction firms, insurers and brokers in the audience. The response was very strong, and AGC worked with Athenium to bring their solution to its member-construction firms with favorable terms for AGC members to help drive adoption.

While this was all going on, things were evolving at AXA XL, which was actually still XL Catlin, as AXA had not come on the scene yet.

Kaplan's team was looking at several tools to help their insureds in the Construction industry, and were piloting a number of them in a similar fashion to what they had done with Athenium. In the midst of all of this pilot activity, AXA acquired XL, which could bring into question the continuation of innovative activities like these, or perhaps just the pausing of them while the dust settles and the new owners of the business decide how and where they want to invest.

AXA Group's CEO, Thomas Buberl, shared a positioning with the global organization that really resonated with Kaplan and his team. Buberl said they wanted to move from being a payer to a partner. As a specialist with deep expertise in the construction space, this was exactly how Kaplan and his team had been operating, and their RRI approach to piloting solutions was about creating a focused partnership with customers around defining the future of both the customer's business and AXA XL's.

In this spirit, Kaplan and his team saw how all of the disparate tools they were trying with customers were valuable, but could have immensely more value to everyone involved if the tools were brought together in a sort of construction ecosystem. While ecosystems are being talked about a lot now, it was still a new idea in 2018 (especially in Commercial and Specialty Lines), and one that required much more understanding before any decisions or plans could be made.

The idea of an ecosystem is one in which a series of tools and providers come together to create a unified offering to the market that has more value as a whole than in pieces. Because the Construction business at AXA XL included nine lines of business, it made for a natural place to try to build an ecosystem because AXA XL had multiple areas to bring in many different tools or could identify individual tools with benefits across a number of areas.

For example, they had been experimenting with a safety-related wearable device to reduce injuries for workers and drive down WC losses. An RRI pilot customer saw the wearable solution as a way to retire the use of self-reported time tracking or clock-punching, reducing both wage theft by employees (a benefit to the insured) and the risk of underpayment on the employer's part (a benefit to the employees and to AXA XL who may avoid an EPL claim as a result). In this way, looking at things as an ecosystem opens you up to a multiplier effect when it comes to benefits you can realize.

Additionally, as more customers join the ecosystem, the data generated through their participation can help the entire ecosystem through things such as powering better prediction (as discussed in the CNA case) and allowing for benchmarking. This last idea was especially valuable to insureds. The only benchmarking that construction firms could do previously was across their own projects. While valuable, it limited their ability to see gaps they had across the board, or spot new ways they could reduce risk to their people, their projects or their own customers.

In early 2019, Gress and Kaplan brought together a number of people from across the Construction business to think about which customers would be ideal for an RRI project around the ecosystem concept. They wanted a mix of customers across different regions and types of construction with different appetites for innovation, and that had as many of AXA XL's nine lines of insurance as possible to maximize the multiplier effect of the benefits available. And they had limited budget with which to do it since this idea did not exist when they were setting their 2019 budget.

With a list of target customers ready, the team started to reach out about participating and putting in place the required legal contracts for the pilot. This provided a good learning to AXA XL about their estimation of the time needed to iron out the legal agreements on how to structure and run a pilot. It was their first time doing this at such scale and complexity. Their past RRI pilots had kicked off so quickly and smoothly, the longer process surprised the team a bit, but they were able to work through it and move forward. Their goal was to have the pilots complete before the next Customer Council, which was in April.

At that event, they had presentations from the technology providers to share with the Council about their solutions. They also had the customers involved in the pilots share their experience and their learnings. Then the AXA XL team presented the concept of an ecosystem to everyone at the Council. It was just a concept since they had no live version of it, merely the idea and tests of some of the pieces of the puzzle. Despite it just being an idea, the reception from the Customer Council was very strong, proving that there was value in it and that it was something that could dramatically push AXA XL deeper into the role of a partner rather than a payer.

After the meeting, they continued pilots, gathering more insight into what the ecosystem needed to be, a single place you log into with interconnected tools and data giving cohesive insights that can be acted on. What was still missing was a way to have really powerful benchmarks. No matter how many amazing technology tools were integrated into the platform, the universe of data was still going to be limited to what AXA XL saw from a loss standpoint and what its insureds saw from their business. There was a need for much more loss data, and AXA XL had a partner they could turn to that could help.

Sedgwick, the third-party administrator (TPA), had significant scale in their business adjusting claims across Workers' Compensation, Property and other construction-related lines of business. While they could not share the raw data, there was a level of it they could make available to AXA XL with specifics such as insured and carrier masked. This allowed for an unmatched ability to give insureds benchmarks that could materially change their business while helping AXA XL's risk engineers support those insureds more effectively at preventing loss.

As the idea kept getting clearer and more refined, Gress and his technology partner in the project, Doug Alexander, AXA XL Digital Architect, worked closely to make it reality. Partnering with IT, which has come up in many cases, is critical to success, and the relationship Gress and Alexander had on this project is a great example of that.

Gress describes Alexander as someone who took an extreme interest in the success of the project. He could have pushed for it to be a purely-internally-built solution, as might have been the case in the past. Instead, he was fully open to finding the best solutions available, and recognized that the world of insurtech companies would be more able to quickly solve for the team's needs, and to do it within-budget. With that partnership leading the project, it was time to build the first version of the ecosystem to bring to market.

At the same time, Kaplan and Gress were also thinking of other applications for the ecosystem and tapped Rose Hall, Strategic Operations Manager for Risk Engineering, with looking at the adoption of technology across their Construction customer base. Hall has led the way in building a model that benchmarks a contractor's level of tech adoption against their peers across several categories of technology, including various devices, systems and software. The team believes that adopting and leveraging technology on construction sites paves the way for safer, more efficient, and ultimately more profitable construction projects in an accelerated and unprecedented manner.

Hall said of the intention behind the work:

"In 2020, in the construction industry, we are still building mostly the same way we have been for decades, with very little innovation, many inefficiencies, and far too many injuries and fatalities. It's time to leverage technology and embrace the devices, systems, and software that can help us solve business problems and save lives. Our goal with this ecosystem and the tech adoption maturity index (TAMI) is to encourage and support that growth into a new era of bigger, better, and safer construction."

As rising waters float all boats, greater industry adoption of technology should foster safer and more efficient operating practices industry-wide, thus driving a reduction in risk, and leading to lower losses over time. The tools in AXA XL's ecosystem technology library are curated to enhance contractors' risk management efforts by predicting, mitigating, and preventing losses. Hall's benchmarking work capitalizes on contractors' ambition for continuous improvement and their inherent competitive nature to encourage technological adoption at an increased pace. That is, by showing contractors how far ahead of them another contractor might be, benchmarking can propel adoption, and thus better business and loss performance.

Hall added more detail on why it has been hard for many in the construction industry to innovate, and how AXA XL can partner with them to do so through the tools in the ecosystem:

"Allowing technology adoption to grow organically in a legacy industry such as construction has historically been a relatively slow transformation. With razor thin margins, many contractors have neither the financial or technical resources to invest in research and development of new technologies, at the same time focusing on safely delivering quality projects on time and on budget. However, if they can rely on their partner in risk (AXA XL) to perform some of the heavy lifting, we can kick-start that evolution by equipping our customers with the tools, resources, and consulting support of our risk engineers to navigate the vast and daunting world of construction tech. This way we all get there much faster."

Hall's TAMI benchmark assessment brings objectivity and science to what has been a subjective measure in the past around tech adoption, which can then have additional uses for AXA XL. By knowing the impact of tech adoption on losses and having a scientific measure of an insured's propensity to adopt technology, AXA XL can then consider this data in developing and modifying their pricing models in the long-term.

The ability to link the technology AXA XL is delivering through its ecosystem to customer behavior is extremely important and will drive adoption, risk selection, risk management, and competitive pricing and products on AXA XL's part.

Unfortunately, this was late in 2019, and the budget was getting low. AXA XL again turned to the team at Athenium, who had proven flexible, incredibly capable, and clearly able to operate in a world of sensitive data and high security standards from their experience with the US intelligence community. They had also built solutions outside of weather that spoke more directly to what AXA XL would need to facilitate the ecosystem idea. As they had in the past, Athenium got into the project quickly, generating a prototype to share with customers.

In November of 2019, the four pilot customers came together with the teams from AXA XL and Athenium to discuss feedback from the pilot, look at screen shots of the proposed system, gauge reactions and see what gaps remained in the concept.

At the same time, Gress and Alexander met with AXA Group CEO Buberl again, who was very supportive of the ecosystem idea. In that meeting, he approved the project, and wanted it to be ready by the annual RIMS conference in May of 2020. With less than $50,000 remaining in the budget, the teams at AXA XL and Athenium dug in, sharing iterations of the solution with six customers to get rapid feedback starting in January of 2020.

The concept featured several key components to start, including the aggregated and anonymized claim benchmarking data that Sedgwick was helping with; a library of recommended technology solutions for specific problems a construction firm may run into (for example, a solution for identifying water leaks before they go too far); project-specific tools to help with bidding, managing projects, etc. and more tools to reduce risk and improve the insured's business results. It also featured enhancements to GaugeConstruction, like an advanced Lightning prediction tool, and a mobile app, which is critical for risk managers who frequently walk job sites rather than staying tethered to a computer screen in an office.

Through this process, one thing that stood out was the legal intricacies of data.

AXA XL's North American General Counsel reviewed the legal issues associated with data ownership, use and privacy. It became clear that all the stakeholders in an ecosystem pilot had their own ideas about data. Getting everyone comfortable on these issues was going to be a key success factor or point of failure for the ecosystem pilot and ultimately the ecosystem as a whole.

AXA XL spent a lot of time talking to their customers and vendors to make sure any proprietary or sensitive aspects of their data were protected during a pilot and thereafter. At the same time, customers and partners had to be willing to grant AXA XL access to certain parts of their data (where legally allowable) to enable the creation of the ecosystem and all of its benefits. While data is a common conversation topic in the technology and insurance worlds, it was not as common in the construction industry, so working through this with customers and vendors was important and needed to be done carefully so everyone knew who owned or had access to what and why. There was clearly room for discomfort in this subject.

One example of this issue in practice comes in a claim scenario. If the data in the ecosystem paints a picture of what happened in the claim, for example that there was a high wind gust at the altitude a worker was at when they fell, this could help dramatically with AXA XL's work in adjusting the WC claim that would follow the accident.

But what if that data showed something the insured thought would paint them in a negative light or expose something they did not want exposed?

AXA XL's response to this is that, overall, the truth should be far more helpful in explaining what happened when and to what or who, so claims can be handled quickly, paid as fast as possible, and workers can get back to work or property can be replaced expeditiously. Could you end up in a situation where the technology shows something AXA XL did not know about? Of course. Might that information be unfavorable to the insured? It might, but it also might show AXA XL something they did not realize that leads to the claim being covered. Since it can cut both ways, it is something insureds and AXA XL would need to get comfortable with together.

The ultimate idea is that more truth helps identify areas to protect against or recover from loss more than give either side something to use against the other.

Of course, not every customer will see it that way, and that is OK. It just means the ecosystem is not right for that customer at this time. Most customers, however, did get comfortable with it.

AXA XL has had a very healthy response to the tools because they have gathered so many proof points and benefits from their RRI projects of different pieces of the ecosystem and through their prototype implementation. And because they have consistently been sharing this with customers and seeking feedback, the understanding of it is definitely further along than if they had kept it a secret, not involving customers in the development of the solution.

When it comes to results, it is still too early to talk about tangible dollars saved or gained. Feedback from GaugeConstruction users has been immensely positive, and the changes Athenium keeps making to their tool to increase usability and enrich the feature set (like the Lightning functionality) will only drive that value up further.

The ecosystem will only have just launched as this book comes out, so it is obviously far too early to talk about the benefit there, but the pilot work implies it will be real. The hope for AXA XL is that loss ratios improve through insureds avoiding losses (for example, not deploying a crane during extreme wind), but also as AXA XL's risk engineers help insureds reduce risk more effectively through the insights they gain from the various tools and benchmarks in the ecosystem. These insights will enable more impactful conversations between risk engineers and customers than they would otherwise be able to have. AXA XL also expects the ecosystem to help on the topline through being a valuable way to earn new business opportunities, and in retaining quality business through being a true business partner rather than just the company who pays when something goes wrong.

While this all sounds like a herculean effort that must have taken an army, Gress laughed when he looked back at how lean they were. The active team on the ecosystem project was just a handful of people: Gress, Alexander, a business analyst on Gress's team, plus some strong resources from IT, Legal and the Business/Risk Engineering Teams who took this on in addition to their full-time roles. Their openness to partnering with companies like Athenium, and other insurtech providers, is definitely part of how and why they were able to get this done as leanly as they did.

They also learned a lot along the way, and have put together something they are not only proud of, but that they are also optimistic can have a dramatic impact on losses *and* the business results of their customers.

They also realize that, as quickly and leanly as they built the ecosystem or launched its components like GaugeConstruction before building the ecosystem, a competitor can still come in and do it faster. That means that you cannot think you are done when you have completed something. You have to stay connected to your customers, hear what issues they face (whether these are insurance-related or not), and stay open to what you might find by exploring each customer's needs with them that you may never have expected.

Foundations for The Future

- Short-duration, focused projects that start with Blue Sky thinking around a problem or opportunity and move to a solution that can be implemented within ninety days can be used to innovate how a business works, but, more importantly, how its customers value it.

- Tight, fixed timelines on projects can avoid the pitfalls and burnout of open-ended projects while the focus they require for delivery keep the team on the project highly-engaged; this can work for longer-term projects by breaking them into a series of smaller segments, as in the Agile approach to development.

- No matter how great your solution is, someone can always do better, so it is important to stay engaged with your customers and adjust as you hear from them on what would make their business better (regardless of how it directly ties to insurance).

10. USAA & The Evolution of Innovation

Almost 100 years ago, a group of officers in the US military decided to do something innovative and solve for a problem they faced. Existing insurance solutions did not provide the flexibility of coverage they needed, especially when deployed overseas, as many Americans had been in World War I, which had only recently ended. They knew it would take a business model of mutual support and understanding that was unique to people in their situation, putting their lives on the line for their country.

I say, "mutual," but they felt the mutual model was not quite enough for the level of connection and support they sought to create for each other, and instead opted for a reciprocal structure whereby insureds effectively insure each other. It was the original peer-to-peer business model, long before the way the Internet facilitated the creation of multiple peer-to-peer businesses (including some carriers purporting to be P2P). That company, of course, is USAA.

After nearly a century, USAA remains a reciprocal, and has also remained deeply dedicated to its mission of serving those who serve. The connection to its core mission and principles has resulted in a focus on its members that many businesses, let alone carriers, talk about but few achieve in practice the way USAA has. That focus has resulted in several benefits to the company, including the highest NPS in the US of any company in any industry, in fact, their insurance and banking businesses are the top two,[20] and a level of mutual trust with its members of which most companies would be envious.

---

[20] Smith, Tom, "Top 10 U.S. Net Promoter Scores (NPS) for 2013."

With that strong mission that resonates throughout USAA's employee base and an innovative mindset behind the company's inception in the first place, there has always been an aspiration to keep pushing forward on how to best-serve the members.

Throughout the company, there is a desire and need to keep evolving and innovating to protect the security of the military community. USAA's members protect the world's freedom every single day. They are the most diverse "business" anywhere and the military continuously innovates to solve problems all the time. USAA is a mirror of their membership, and in fact 25% of USAA's employees are military veterans or their spouses. Again, many companies recognize the need to continuously innovate, but USAA has the proof behind how widespread this desire is through things like patents the company has been awarded. If you look at the more-than-1,000 patents issued to USAA, you will find specific employees named in the filings as the source of the idea on the overwhelming majority. You might expect these to be technical people, or staff in innovation-focused roles, but in fact they span every function. Famously, a security guard at the company's headquarters is named in twenty-five of their patents. USAA has built a giant art installation of a tree where each leaf names an employee and the patent they are credited with leading to so as to further celebrate and foster the innovative mindset across the organization.

In addition to the patent program, USAA fosters a culture of innovation through their Employee Innovation program. Each year more than 90% of employees participate in the program by submitting, voting on, and championing ideas. Consideration is given to cost/benefit, employee and member experience, resource requirements, and compliance and regulatory requirements with a focus on implementing the most impactful ideas in the business.

Top management consulting firms have often talked about the core ingredients of having an innovative culture in your company,[21] and USAA has benefited from those table-stakes items. Three of the most often-cited ingredients to successful innovation are:

---

[21] Deloitte, "In pursuit of innovation, A CEO checklist," January, 2015; "Developing a resilient, innovative organizational culture – Considerations for the board," December 2015.

1. Having leadership that is bought into innovation.
2. Protecting the innovation function.
3. Protecting the innovation budget.

With these principles, and the company's and its employee's dedication to its mission in place, USAA created a central Innovation team that has moved the ball forward in a number of areas across their businesses.

With their Labs unit, they are connected to stakeholders both internally and externally to get and share ideas, include members in the testing and refinement process of those ideas, and bring some truly innovative solutions to market. Their work keeps them abreast of competitive activities as well as the development of new technologies and solutions beyond what their competitors are doing to see if they might be of value to USAA or its members.

Those efforts resulted in a number of pioneering solutions, such as being the first to use scans of checks for remote deposit by members who bank with USAA and then moving to using their mobile app to capture check images before anyone else. It also resulted in the creation of their interactive catastrophe map, which they built as a response to Hurricane Harvey as it devasted Houston and other areas. After the storm hit, various people from across the organization came together to design, build and deploy, in a single day, a web tool so members (and ultimately anyone) could see if their home was impacted by the storm, and if so, how badly.

Yet despite the success USAA was having with its ability to innovate, and the despite the benefits to its members, they realized that using their approach to innovation to change how they serve their members is not enough. They also need to innovate *how* they innovate. That is, they recognized that even the idea of innovation must evolve.

What they realized is that they were sometimes taking an interesting, emerging technology and trying to fit it into their existing business model. There is certainly value in being aware of emerging technology and thinking long-term about it, but that practice can also lead to a lack of delivery on things that move the business forward because you struggle to find a clear purpose for the technology or a meaningful way to implement it that resonates with customers.

This is the dynamic behind many technologies that were "before their time" like the Apple Newton, the original electric cars (from the

1890s) or the GM EV1, and more.[22] More specific to insurance, several carriers jumped on the idea of Blockchain and what it might be able to do, but did not have a specific idea of how and where to implement it, making it less inherently-valuable, as evidenced by the relative paucity of applications in the industry today. USAA, as we will see later, took a different approach to using Blockchain, which resulted in material value from the technology.

A decision was made by the company's leadership in early 2017 to change their approach to innovation. They kept the existing, centralized Innovation function, but decided to augment it. The idea was that, in addition to exploration of emerging technologies, innovation needs to start with a very specific problem to ensure that what is developed is useful for and valuable to members.

This means needing to be closer to the members and employees in each of USAA's businesses to identify and understand the problems being faced, which required embedding innovation units within the business. For P&C, this includes the Auto Product, Property Product and Claims units, who would start up innovation teams.

Ramon Lopez was selected to build and lead the Claims Innovation team by CCO Sean Burgess. The various teams working on innovation across the business would not be in competition with each other or the central Innovation team, but rather stay focused on the problems in their area while coming back together to collaborate on cross-functional or broader issues and support each other's efforts.

USAA was essentially creating an innovation ecosystem whereby the central and business-specific innovation teams would join up on a regular cadence along with the company's CVC unit to review each of their portfolios, update each other on progress, give feedback and support, and collaborate on shared ideas. The portfolios being discussed were portfolios of problems rather than technologies or solutions. That meant that, if a particular technology ended up not being a viable solution to a problem, the technology would drop out of the portfolio but the problem would remain in it. This ensured an ongoing focus on members' needs in every idea the teams worked on rather than that focus being risked by technologies succeeding or

---

[22] Love, Dylan, "8 Inventions That Were Way Ahead of Their Time," Business Insider, July 2, 2013.

failing.

For Claims, Lopez assembled people from within and outside of the function, as did his peers setting up other Innovation teams. The way they assembled their teams was critical to their success. Lopez sought a mix of military veterans and spouses (over 25% of the team), Claims expertise, technical expertise, insurance experience and non-insurance talent that had lived in the startup world. Some came from successful startups, while others had learned a great deal from businesses that had not made it. It was important to bring all perspectives into the mix. Each team member had to operate like a CEO: they must know the financials; be able to operate in a cross-functional organization; be able to market and tell the story of their idea so that the innovations they develop are supported and successful; etc.

One of the people who joined the Claims Innovation team early on is Luke Harris, who came from outside the company. He shared some of the drivers on why innovation has thrived in Claims at USAA, especially since this shift in approach in 2017. On top of the type of people that came together in the team, Harris talked specifically about three Claims Innovation foundational philosophies as central to everything they do and how they do it.

They are:
1. Be Actively Transparent.
2. Build Trust.
3. Take Extreme Ownership.

Be Actively Transparent

While innovation functions in some companies operate in the dark as a sort of skunkworks, Claims Innovation at USAA decided not to follow this approach. Instead, Harris stressed how they feel strongly that you need to be open and actively engage with your internal and external stakeholders. If you try to build something in a vacuum without bringing your stakeholders along, it is much harder to get the solution into production and have it truly have impact because of all the valuable feedback and support you miss along the way by staying dark.

Instead, Claims Innovation at USAA brings their stakeholders along with a view of what problem they are trying to solve to see if the proposed idea really helps and, if so, how best to move it forward. They take in feedback, adjust what they are doing, and stay connected to those stakeholders throughout the process.

"Innovation fails if you build something and throw it over the fence to someone and expect them to use it."

– Luke Harris
AVP, Claims Innovation, USAA

Being open and inclusive of stakeholders also helps firm up how to deliver the idea into production. This helps expose what needs to exist for training, deployment, etc. It also gives the team a chance to tell the story of the product or innovation so it is not a surprise to anyone when it comes out. This helps unlock all the resources that may be needed for the innovation to be a success, such as IT, people in the business, the marketing team, etc.

Harris shared wise advice that, "innovation fails if you build something, throw it over the fence to someone and expect them to use it." He went further on this idea of sharing as a driver of trust, which is the next pillar. Specifically, being transparent by sharing those endeavors that do not work out is as important as sharing those that do. Showing that you are willing to take risks and that you can learn from those that do not work out tells people to be brave, and that they can believe that what you tell them is the whole story rather than just the parts of it that make you look good.

Build Trust

Building from this transparent approach, Harris talked about the intention behind it being about trust. The Claims Innovation team seeks to have trust across not just the entire team itself, but more broadly across any stakeholder they have or may have. People need to trust the team to be willing to invest in what the team is doing.

Beyond the trust the Claims Innovation team needs internally, it is crucial that members trust what they put out, too, or adoption of new ideas will be challenged. As discussed above, USAA has the benefit of a high level of trust from its member base, which serves them well in a number of ways.

Something they have done for a long time is open up their initiatives through their USAA Labs to members, allowing members to participate in testing new solutions the teams are working on. This is about transparency and trust-building.

Those members participating in new ideas will likely trust USAA more by being on the inside of their efforts, but also because the learnings the various Innovation teams get from including members in these efforts helps ensure what is ultimately released sustains or even builds the trust of the member base as a whole, because of how much better the solution is through the impact of that early feedback.

Harris stressed how the team is critically aware of the fragility of trust, and value and respect it highly. Members have been very innovative and willing to try new things USAA offers them because of that trust. That is, members have come to know that what new tools or solutions USAA gives them are going to be helpful and valuable. The team understands that trust is much easier to lose than it is to earn, so you must respect and protect it. People are always going to question why you are not moving faster or if you are working on the right things, but high member trust helps fend off these doubts.

The way the teams see it according to Harris is that members are going to get USAA's trust, but USAA has to earn and keep their member's trust.

Take Extreme Ownership

Leadership expert Jocko Willink[23] is the source of this philosophy that USAA's Claims Innovation team adopted. If every person on the team takes ownership of anything, whether it is within the realm of their control or not, the team will be successful. You may not be the person who is going to solve every problem, but you need to be willing to come to the table to try to solve every problem. This includes problems that fall outside your remit. Every employee needs to be willing to

---

[23] Willink, Jocko and Leif Babin, Extreme Ownership, St. Martin's Press, New York, 2017.

step in and give support well outside what they would feel is in their traditional job responsibilities. While each person should know their role and have clarity in what it entails, if the team needs anything, everyone should be willing to step in and give support.

This is the kind of energy and attitude behind things such as the catastrophe maps that USAA built and released in a day. It is also the spirit that drove the organization's ability to rapidly virtualize their operation when COVID-19 made it imperative to do so. The innovations that made that possible were in development, but scheduled to take several months before they were ready, yet with this extreme ownership mentality, USAA was able to deploy the necessary capabilities within a week.

As Harris says, each member of the team owns strategy and they all own putting it into action tactically, even if they are not directly or explicitly responsible for either.

While it may be clear that USAA has strong values and a mission statement that resonates throughout the organization, none of that matters if these things do not positively impact what they do. While their evolved version of how they innovate is only in the early part of its third year of existence, there has been a clear impact on what USAA has been able to achieve so far.

Starting with the portfolio refocus, Harris shared that roughly 35% (12-15) of existing projects were culled in 2019 as being more focused on a technology than on solving a specific problem. This allowed them to put greater attention and resource on addressing things that would ultimately help members.

The team recognizes that ruthless prioritization and the velocity at which initiatives advance through, or fall out of, the stages of development are critical to their success. Failing fast, or more accurately, "learning fast" is celebrated by the team when objective, data-driven decisions are made to discontinue an initiative. You will often hear the phrase "speed matters" when teammates discuss the problems they are solving.

The portfolio includes projects with different delivery or impact horizons, including many in the near-term, but also some longer-term projects. The balance of near and projects that are three, five or more years from fruition allows USAA to keep looking at the horizon to think about where the industry may go, or how members' needs may change. For example, we are still quite a way from people not owning cars or being driven by autonomous vehicles, but for a major auto insurer such as USAA, that is not a subject to address after it has happened. This is a question they need to think about today, even if the exact timing of things is unclear.

Some of the potential "technology for technology's sake" ideas that you may have expected to drop off became tools to solve for specific problems. One such technology is Blockchain. The problem it is being used to address is around subrogation, where carriers like USAA engage in multiple transactions every day with a variety of other carriers and entities. Many of these transactions end up going back and forth between the same two entities and could potentially have equal but opposite transactions offsetting each other.

Today, there is no way to see the potential for two transactions to cancel each other out, meaning there is a great deal of wasted effort. For example, if USAA owes Carrier X $1,000 for one claim and Carrier X owes USAA $1,000 for another claim, the two should just cancel out and neither carrier should go through the trouble of requesting or fulfilling payment. While it seems obvious, this has never been possible, so insurers end up going through large volumes of basic transactions with each other every day.

Blockchain can be used as a distributed, secure ledger, which is precisely what would be needed to create a central clearing house for subrogation activities between carriers.

In 2018, USAA decided to partner with State Farm to see if they could collaborate on a solution for subrogation payments between the two companies. They did not stop there, though, and thought even further into the future to see if such a solution could be made available to the entire industry (as USAA did with its catastrophe map solution).

After a series of phases to the project, USAA's and State Farm's joint effort has shown that roughly 80% of transactions and dollars transferred could be reduced each day through this approach, which obviously would have a huge impact on industry efficiency. Rather than pay each other each time, the two carriers use their Blockchain ledger to process a single transaction that is the net value owed between each other each day. Whereas the two carriers may have had thousands of transactions per year between them, they would only have roughly 250 (one per business day).

If this was to be adopted across other carriers, the impact becomes massive. Extrapolating out, I estimate that $4.7 billion and roughly 1.4 million transactions could be saved across the US P&C industry annually. [24]

Another area the team has innovated in involves adjusting auto claims fully-digitally with self-service tools. Partnering with Google Cloud, USAA has developed tools for insureds to capture images of their vehicle after an accident, upload them into the cloud for near-real-time processing to generate an estimate of the damage and the cost of repair on the spot.

I remember when my family was rear-ended, taking photos of my car in my insurer's mobile app, and then waiting about six days before a final estimate was ready from the body shop for me to know if I would ever see my car again (or if I would want to given the extent of the damage). The process was not painful *per se*, but it was longer than I expected it to be, was fraught with several missteps along the way that slowed it down (for example, my last name was misspelled when it was transmitted to the body shop, so that slowed things down as they could not start the work since they did not have a work order tied to the banged up car I left on their lot). Not knowing about the extent of the damage, whether the car was totaled or if my sense of the damage fit what the estimate would ultimately state created stress and anxiety at an already high-stress time. Had I seen details of and repair cost for the damage on the spot, I can safely say this would have dramatically changed my claim experience. And for the carrier, this would save them a great deal of phone tag with me, the body shop and anyone else involved. It could also result in fewer rental car days or other ancillary benefits to the insurer on top of the much better customer experience this creates.

Because the innovation process that lead to the solution was inclusive of various stakeholders, including members, USAA created a flexible solution. The intention for USAA is not to force members into one service channel or another. Their adjusters are always there for members if needed, and no one *has* to use the AI-powered adjusting

---

[24] Pirus, Benjamin, "State Farm and USAA See Stark Increase in Efficiency When Testing Blockchain Subrogation," Forbes, July 18, 2019.

process, or stay with it if they started that way.

The company's goal in all of its Claims innovations is to deliver a connected, empathetic and effortless claim member experience. They want there to be little to no additional effort for their members to have their claim resolved seamlessly and in a personalized manner to meet their needs. That means having both a digital and adjuster path, based on what members want. And with the right digital tools, USAA would naturally see a shift to more automation without having to force members in that direction. Like earning and keeping trust, USAA tries to build solutions that earn and keep members' adoption. This then allows their people to really focus in on delivering the "empathetic" part of the goal because of the time the digital tools save adjusters on the process side.

USAA is not the only carrier doing this type of digital, AI-powered adjusting. It does standout that they worked with a non-traditional partner, Google, to power such a solution, though. This, and the State Farm partnership on subrogation, are examples of one of the ways USAA believes evolution will take place in the industry; through partnerships, including non-traditional ones.

Working with a major (and the largest) competitor is not a traditional or standard approach. Working with Google would not be the first thought many in the industry might have when considering a cloud computing solution for an insurance application, even if it is the best for this application. Whether the partner is obvious or traditional or not, USAA is clear that partnerships will be crucial to the future of insurance.

Harris also credits the make-up of their Innovation teams, being so diverse in terms of backgrounds, perspectives and strengths, as another key to how he sees the industry being able to evolve. Having a group of people with insurance and non-insurance backgrounds ensures you get core subject matter expertise combined with outside perspectives and an inherent need to ask questions to understand a situation, which may unlock solutions that would not have been possible with people from a single type of background. The same is true with the functional and technical background differences on the team.

The final point Harris made that has helped drive their success is for the entire Innovation team to not look at innovation as the destination. This means they all serve their time in the team, but then are encouraged to take what they have learned to the broader business.

In this way, the Innovation function will export talent into the business that has had time looking over the horizon.

The example from USAA is different in that it is not about any one solution. Instead, it is a valuable case to close with because it reminds us that even innovation must evolve. We may be having a profound impact on our organization through the way we apply new ideas, but there will likely be opportunities to shift how we engage in this journey. USAA will no doubt adjust their approach to innovation again in the future, and again after that.

What does not change, however, is the guiding idea of serving those who serve. They were courageous in not being content with their success as an innovator in P&C, banking and their other businesses as they recognized there is always a need to keep up with and even step ahead of how your customers' needs shift if you want to truly serve them.

Foundations for The Future

- Being problem-focused can ensure innovative efforts are well-spent on things that genuinely improve the business and the customer experience.

- Diverse teams who see every problem as one they should care about and try to help with creates a supportive, inclusive culture of innovation with those directly tasked with it, but also more broadly across an innovative organization as a whole.

- Do not be content with current success in innovation to keep it from dying out, and instead stay open to new approaches to how you stay relevant to customers whose needs will continue to evolve.

III. MOVING FORWARD

While the cases above provide valuable insight into how we can move forward, the question remains whether we still can. Do we have the tools we need? Have we missed our chance?

If the discussion and cases above do not answer these last two questions clearly enough for you, Rob Galbraith made it clear that now is the time to think about moving forward as we have the means and the opportunity. He said, "The core technologies that can disrupt the P&C insurance industry exist now. It will take time, money, people and ingenuity to translate these technologies into meaningful change in the industry."[25]

With the enabling technology solutions available to us, and a shift in the balance of power from incumbent to startup carriers not having occurred, now is the time to evolve. From the cases above, three themes become clear as we look across all of the Foundations for the Future:

1. Customers hold the answer.
2. Engage your people.
3. Be focused on intention, outcome and time.

We will look at each of them in turn in this section, starting with a focus on customers.

---

[25] Galbraith, pg. 336.

11. Customers Hold the Answer

A consistent theme throughout the cases in this book is one of listening to what customers are asking for. In cases where this did not come up, there was no opposing or contradicting message.

As Jeff Goldberg from Novarica shared, "it is important to get direct feedback from customers without interpretation or filtering between you and them. Customers will tell you what they wish was different, how they want to work with you, and how adjacent things in their business or their lives could be made better by your work."

CSAA talked to customers directly to develop their idea around substituting ride sharing for rental cars. They listened to customers on issues with the current offering, but, more importantly, CSAA stepped back from the immediate problem at hand to understand customers' lives more broadly. The notion of trying to solve for how customers get from Point A to Point B when they cannot use their own car does not come from thinking of your own world (offering rental cars) and then asking how to fix one part of it or another. CSAA put themselves in the customer's shoes to frame the conversation, and then let customers describe the situation themselves rather than guessing at what they might want.

CNA's work on evolving their approach to finding fraud may not sound like something that comes from the customers. In reading the case, you will see several points where the customer's (or injured worker's) needs clearly came into play in designing a solution. CNA's sensitivity to lengthening the process while investigating a claim they would not have flagged for potential fraud in the past is a clear focus on customer needs. Reducing fraud itself has customer-centric benefits around keeping rates lower and helping get people healthy and returning their lives to normal faster, which is what everyone hopes for when they have suffered a loss.

Not keeping this customer view in mind could lead to a much more aggressive approach to fraud (and I have seen carriers do that in presuming every claim is fraudulent from the start).

SCIF's use of Design Thinking training and projects means every associate starts with a customer need or problem when looking for new ideas or solutions. Robinson and Anthony were honest that the company had not been thinking about their direct customers in their prior approach to selling direct, treating them like brokers or agents.

The simple recognition that customers need help, while brokers want to transact reframed the basis of their engagement in the move to quote and bind online.

Vern Steiner's desire to have not just fewer questions in the application, but as few as possible with no exceptions or gray areas was directly informed by the difficulty and frustration direct buyers had when they simply needed to protect their workers and meet requirements placed on them for coverage. The things SCIF learned through their approach of seeing the process through the eyes of their direct customers is even feeding into their broker business, because of their openness to what people outside the company are experiencing.

For Ohio Mutual, customers literally told them what they wanted, over and over. And the team was relentless despite difficulties and failed attempts at solving for customers' desire to text until they finally found something that really pleased customers and their staff. They could have stopped at the second-to-last solution they tested since it helped OMIG, but because they kept their ear to the ground on what customers thought, and because of Russell's focus on needing to earn the business and loyalty of every customer they serve, "good enough" was not good enough if it left customers hanging. Because of how they solved for that need for more flexible, real-time communication, they have created a pathway into even more feedback from customers about what they want and how they feel about working with OMIG.

EMPLOYERS started with a different definition of "customer" than many carriers do by not forcing a choice between insureds and distributors. They realized that they cannot serve one of these constituents at the expense of the needs of the other, which meant listening to those needs and solving for both if they were to survive today, and thrive in a changed market tomorrow.

Dirks instilled this across his leadership team, and treated his people like customers by being honest and open with them, and giving them space for their ideas to come to the surface and be pursued. Their API idea has been as successful as it is because of the way they have engaged with their customers, taking in feedback constantly, making customers part of the design process, and adjusting what they build as they hear about needs changing from their distributors or from how end-insureds are using their tools.

For AXA XL, their use of the RRI approach to evolving their offering is heavily-focused on the inclusion of customers in the process. Using their Customer Council and sharing openly with these customers before they even have an idea fully vetted allows customers to give feedback and guidance so that whatever AXA XL works on speaks to the genuine needs of customers.

To solve for those needs using the RRI methodology is another example of listening to and caring for your customer's needs because the structure of the projects makes it easier for customers to engage given the clarity of scope and timelines of the projects. This creates so many points of value for customers and AXA XL. If you are able to step back from a specific need to reduce losses, you see how helping your customer win bids or not lose money on those they do win means that insured is likely to renew with you and have a growing business with better loss performance, making them a stronger account to cover for the long-term. Without the baked-in customer feedback of RRI, AXA XL would likely not offer tools to help their insureds thrive as businesses beyond just their ability to manage risk.

Going one step further for AXA XL, the Construction business has a vision statement that guides what they do. It explicitly talks about partnering with top contractors, so the notion of working closely with customers is literally at the heart of the business.

Lastly, it is no secret that has been newly-revealed in this book that USAA is intensely focused on their members. This was reiterated time and time again in the story of how they reshaped what had been an already-successful approach to innovation. They ensured a keen focus on members' problems as the definition for everything in their innovation portfolio. They stay connected to members throughout the innovation process, include them along the way, and are committed to the idea of serving those who serve to the point that USAA rethinks how they are innovating to ensure they do not fall behind what those members' evolving needs are.

In case after case, it is clear that having your customer in mind is the right start. Going a step further by actually involving them in your solution-building process is where these examples stand apart, and where the takeaway advice lies.

12. Engage Your People

While there are components of many of these cases that feature top-down decisions or direction, what no case exhibits is success purely from a top-down approach. In example after example, you see how the involvement, dedication and support of the people is why they succeeded.

At CSAA, while several people worked on the project and the Executives in charge approved the work, that was not enough. From the early ideation which included front-line Claims staff, to the time the project team spent with various people across different levels and rolls throughout the organization to ensure people were bought in, gave their feedback, and were ready for the change, success was about engaging with the people.

Beyond that, the project team camped out in the Claims call center to be with the internal people effected by the new idea (and hear first-hand as customers reacted to it). Any other way of doing this may have "worked", but the team would have missed so many nuances that lead to its success. That could mean they did not pick up on ways to make it resonate with insureds better or perhaps ideas to make for a smoother process. They also may have unintentionally created resistance to the idea from people who felt left-out or blindsided by the change, making it harder for the ride sharing solution to succeed.

Leaders at CNA Claim could have simply gone out and gotten a new fraud solution and told their people to use it. They could have worked with Shift through the thirty-day development cycles without involving staff from the SIU. They could have ignored the need to support their people throughout the SIU and Claim team more broadly with training, or to get feedback from those using the tool directly to see whether it was working or how to make things work better after it went live. And doing things this way may have been fine.

In fact, this may have been the approach used at many carriers in the past (or even still today). Instead, Rob Thomas and his team actively involved multiple SIU team members, data scientists, training and change specialists and more. They sought out feedback from their people constantly, and if the solution was not working for those people, the project team went back to Shift to see if something could be done about it or made an internal change themselves. Involving so many people in so many ways is a critical part of why the solution has been embraced internally as it has been and why CNA has seen such success with it.

SCIF engaged all of their people in its evolution, without exception. The idea for online Quote and Bind for direct customers did not originate from the people, however, as it was one of the strategic imperatives Steiner and his leadership team developed and initiated. Despite starting that way, it quickly was given to the people to move forward on as they needed to, gathering feedback and input from across functions and roles.

The solution itself has had a tremendous impact on the people working on direct business as they feel a sense of purpose and value in the company that was not clear before having the investment in creating a strong flow of new business into the company. And as Steiner said, while the nature of having civil servants and union employees may require a company to be open with and involving of its staff, they would have done it this way regardless because of how crucial that engagement is to truly evolving.

Claims staff at Ohio Mutual have been engaged in finding a way to solve for customers' desire to text for a long time. They have been willing to try many different approaches to the problem. The company chose, however, not to use several of those approaches because of the burden they placed on their staff (such as the shared BlackBerry approach). And even with their use of Hi Marley, where they find some associates who are more hesitant to adopt the tool, they have not issued an edict or order that everyone has to use it. Instead, when they see lower usage, they offer a helping hand to that employee to help overcome their hesitation.

The views of the staff have mattered throughout OMIG's texting journey, and their approach to evolving the company overall. The three teams Russell created to move the company forward around continuous improvement, customer satisfaction and agent engagement all involve people from across the organization who stay in their day jobs expressly because that is a way to keep the needs of the people in each function front and center through OMIG's work to evolve.

For EMPLOYERS, Dirk's engagement with the staff about the new way they were looking at ideas and the direction for the company sent a clear message that every idea is worth sharing, and the best ones will get supported.

Chris Champlin shared how he felt supported and like he and his peers had a voice to raise their ideas up for consideration, which has unlocked growth engines that are driving EMPLOYERS' expansion and success nationally. People not only understand where the company is going, but feel free and encouraged to contribute to that direction in any area they have an idea regardless of what they do at the company.

AXA XL Construction has ensured everyone in the business does at least one RRI project each year, meaning everyone is a part of either solving a problem the business faces or grabbing an opportunity in front of it. That engagement means people feel valued, and, in return, contribute meaningfully to moving the business forward. While that sentiment may sound familiar to many employees at different carriers who do not see it playing out in actuality, the way AXA XL Construction has innovated in their market and been supported all the way up to the CEO of AXA globally sends a message that this is more than just talk, and the contribution of each individual genuinely matters. That Justin Gress joked about how small the team at AXA XL was that was working on the ecosystem is a sign of the dedication they all put into it because they know their efforts matter and will have impact.

Going back to AXA XL Construction's vision statement I referenced earlier, not only does it mention customers explicitly, but it is actually about the Construction *team* rather than the business, putting the focus on the people themselves. AXA XL Construction could not achieve what they have as quickly as they have without this mentality.

USAA engages its people on a variety of levels and ways across its approach to innovation. They have made explicit efforts around this, from assembling innovation teams from across and beyond the organization, to encouraging and supporting the generation of ideas by any employee who may end up with a leaf on the Innovation Tree, to the extreme transparency and honesty their innovation teams live by to ensure stakeholders are openly involved and informed. With a shared commitment around members, USAA takes that internal alignment to be a license to include anyone who wants to take extreme ownership of a problem members are facing.

Regardless of the context, every success story hinges on the work of employees who feel empowered and engaged in their company's evolution. That is how culture is shifted to create lasting change and lasting ability to change. The leaders in these cases saw that, and ensured their people were not just along for the journey, but were the ones driving the car with a sense of the direction in which the organization overall needed to go.

13. Be Focused on Intention, Outcome & Time

If there is one lesson that applies universally to any story of successful innovation, it is around focus. The draw of shiny objects around us can be incredibly strong, and can come from many well-intentioned sources: articles we read, colleagues and friends in the industry, customers, advisors, boards, consultant, investors, competitors, partners and more.

This lesson applies not just to carriers trying to evolve, but also to startups where the pressure to chase interesting ideas from trusted sources can be difficult to control and contain. The interest in these ideas is also not a bad thing as it can be the source of inspiration and market-changing insights. Stifling this tendency can be another form of headwind for anyone trying to innovate. The cases in this book help bring clarity to how to strike this balance, and in which specific areas to do so.

CSAA makes a point of letting ideas rise up from internal and external sources, and allows both its Strategy & Innovation and CVC teams the space to evaluate these ideas for consideration by the business. And once an idea has been selected to move forward, as with the ride sharing example, they continue to allow room for new ideas to come into the mix on that particular project. However, the scope of what is being delivered is clear, so these ideas are either adjustments or nuances to the path they have embarked on, or game changers that tell them this is not an idea to continue to pursue (that is the pilot would show them that the idea was not viable). New ideas cannot pull them off course completely.

With the ride sharing example, there were many things they learned along the way, and they adjusted, but you did not see them making wholesale changes to what they were building.

For example, as the pilot got off the ground and they started to get feedback on what was resonating with insureds, they kept certain parameters open for adjusters to work within.

A different approach would be to create fixed parameters, but whipsaw back and forth as new insights came in, for example offering one amount in Lyft vouchers one day, then another amount the next because someone gave an opposing view. Or perhaps starting with a fixed geographic area to run the pilot in, having an insured who could have really benefitted from the solution outside of the geography, and suddenly deciding to go nation-wide, creating great strain on their staff who did not yet have the tools or training to support such a sudden shift in scope.

CSAA had an idea, approach, timeline and goal in mind. They stayed true to that, adjusted along the way where they could within those parameters, and noted things that could be too large a change to take on yet for future consideration. They developed a solution that appealed to customers and could be delivered efficiently by both CSAA and Lyft so it could be scaled up across the book and evolved over time.

CNA did the same thing with their work on fraud with Shift Technology. Once the project was underway with one line of business, they saw that project through to delivery. Only when success gates they had determined at the outset with Shift were met did they start the next line of business. Having clear scope, timelines and deliverables spelled out before the work began allowed them to manage what became the concurrent delivery of fraud models with Shift across Auto and WC on time and on budget.

Their work on WC is a great example of seeing areas where the model could be expanded as they moved toward production, but they handled that expansion into things like compensability without derailing the delivery that was already underway so as to protect the project as a whole. CNA adjusted as new information came in while staying clear on what they were delivering when and for what purpose.

The team at SCIF had a sizable effort in front of them to remake the application, quote and bind processes into a faster, more customer-centric experience, which required a lot of work on how they approached new business overall.

There are many tools out there to aid in different aspects of the new business process, including third party data solutions. It would have been easy to go off on tangents evaluation other ways to gather information on prospects without having to ask them for it directly. Doing so would likely have yielded an equally-simple application process to where SCIF landed, but also would have divided the team's attention, extended the project's timing as they evaluated different providers and worked on how to integrate their solutions, and would have increased operating costs.

Instead, SCIF diligently worked through the tough problem they took on to change how they think about evaluating prospective insureds, and let the timeline and intention push their thinking in a focused manner.

In that way, they were able to scale their question set back by roughly 80% in a short amount of time. This allowed their IT efforts to move forward on time, and ensured they were live in market to start capturing the impressive growth they have now seen through their direct channel.

Ohio Mutual was clear from the start on the scope of what they were looking to solve for. While they refined it through the various attempts they made at offering a way for customers to text during a claim, they were always looking for the same solution; a two-way texting solution that allowed them to interact with customers naturally and familiarly while not creating financial or regulatory risks for the business.

Once their goal looked to be in sight with Hi Marley, they had specific timing set for evaluation of the solution, specific people to involve in a specific part of the business, and stayed true to that. They could have added complexities and other ideas into the mix, such as testing payment solutions through text, adding Property adjusters to the AMD pilot users, or moving the goal line in terms of what made for a successful pilot or not. All of those things may have value, but also would have muddied OMIG's ability to evaluate and decide on a solution for their customers' long-standing request to text with them. Once that is in place, there is room for new ideas built on the new position they have moved to.

EMPLOYERS' use of the Agile methodology is a clear example of staying laser focused on scope, time and process. Rather than trying to build everything they might ever need from the start, Champlin and his team sought to answer one or two key questions with a single distribution partner in a fixed period of time. And when new requests came in from the partners they were talking to, rather than shifting development with each new idea, they checked it against the greater ecosystem's needs to gauge overall value and priority against other ideas being proposed.

By following an Agile approach, they were able to evaluate new ideas and slot them in for delivery without upsetting existing development because the short-duration, tight-focus of Agile sprints ensures you will have time soon enough to start on the next idea without disrupting what is already in flight and valuable to deliver.

AXA XL cited the defined scope, time and goalposts of the RRI approach specifically as why they have been successful in their quest to evolve how the construction industry manages risk. They repeatedly hear from customers working on pilots with them how the clear, consistent timelines are helpful at ensuring engagement while minimizing long-term disruption; knowing when they can provide feedback and make adjustments gives them confidence that the right solution will be delivered ultimately and clarity of what success looks like helps them know if things are working out and worth pursuing more broadly.

When new ideas come up, as they have done several times in AXA XL's ecosystem journey, rather than disrupting what is going on, those ideas become new RRI projects, with a specific structure to how they are vetted, developed and delivered. This focus is not just valuable for the type of evolution AXA XL is going through in bringing their ecosystem to market, but even in establishing the Construction business in the first place.

For USAA, a major driver of project focus came from the move to ensure the entire portfolio of projects is about problems faced by members and the business units serving them. This removed the ambiguity of time and intention that can be inherent in letting a technology be a project rather than a way to meet a particular need. Had they continued to support the 30% of the portfolio that was not focused on members' problems, they would have invested time, money and people that could have otherwise been put to directly benefit of the one thing the company holds above all else, its members.

This cleared the space and the resources to achieve even more, and ensure whatever issue they are focused on, even one that has unclear timing and details such as a shift away from individual car ownership, can get the attention it needs to find a meaningful solution.

Clarity and focus are not always easy to have, to stay true to, or to get right upfront when defining a path forward. Being closed to new thinking to protect your focus is also not a wise path as you could miss something critical or avoid going too far down the wrong path before it's too late.

Each of these carriers has ensured they embarked on their idea to evolve in a focused way, while staying open to learning. Rather than leaving it at simply being open, each one of them has a path for what is discovered through that openness, whether adjusting their current delivery, or looking at their next focused effort to address what has come to light.

14. Final Thoughts on Evolution

Regardless of what area your business feels a need to evolve in, or what solutions or partners you enlist in that effort, we as an industry have the capacity for change.

Each of us faces many hurdles standing in the way of our path, and we are not the only ones trying to move forward. Some look like us on the surface while others look different, appearing to have advantages we wish we had. Regardless of appearances and perceptions, we all face the same customer expectations, regulations, talent pool, weather events and more. Whether anything else between us is a barrier to our success is up to us, and the cases we explored here are fantastic reminders that the future is a place we are all heading. Evolving to it from the strongest foundation possible is a choice we can all make.

In my view, evolution will occur in all areas of P&C, though there are some pockets that seem more obvious than others. For example, when people think about innovation, the first thought they have is usually around new ideas in Personal lines or core Commercial lines like usage-based insurance (UBI) in Auto, IoT for Homeowners and Commercial Property insurance, drones for adjusting property losses, AI adjusting of Auto losses, etc. However, as we saw in the cases in this book, there are evolutionary actions going on across the board. New ideas in rating, claims adjusting, customer service, finance, distribution interactions and even the products themselves can and will come to market in all lines and market segments.

I am often asked which types of carriers are more innovative, flexible or likely to be push the envelope. The answer is, "All of them can be." I have seen large carriers many presume will be too hierarchical or political to move quickly do exactly that. I have seen small carriers many assume lack the resources to make an innovative splash use their small size as an advantage to generate and commercialize their ideas rapidly, seeing growth and financial performance gains as a result. Similarly, mid-sized carriers who may seem stuck in the middle do some very creative things to move their business forward. This book contains examples of all of these situations.

A similar question is often posed around what kind of structure is ideal for innovation, or if particular structures make it harder to evolve. Again, every structure has its plusses and minuses, and I have seen success and struggle with all of them. There is no magic answer, nor is there an inherent barrier to evolving solely from being mutual, reciprocal, stock, private, captive or any other structure.

With such opportunity open to players across lines, structures and sizes, going forward, I do not think there is a single type of player that will win or lose, or whether those terms even matter. I do not see it as a question of whether startup carriers will win against incumbents, or vice versa. There is room for both to succeed, and both camps will see some who do not make it. This is not new, nor is it news. As an industry, different players have come and gone for different reasons, while the industry has remained and moved forward. I believe firmly that this situation is no different.

A historical pattern we have seen in Insurance and other industries will continue to repeat itself here. By this, I mean we will see many of the successful innovative startups get acquired by larger, established players seeking to evolve by incorporating new ideas, people and approaches into their business.

This was the path for a prior generation of startup carriers with Esurance getting acquired by Allstate (and now the brand has been retired completely) or Validus and Blackboard being acquired by AIG (with AIG subsequently deciding to wind down Blackboard). We saw the same thing more recently with UK-based Simply Business getting acquired by Travelers just as they were setting up their US operation.

Some of those acquirers will not be incumbent insurers, but may well be incumbent *re*insurers. The reinsurance community has been very supportive of startup carriers from a capacity standpoint, so it would be a natural combination since there is an existing understanding of the startup's book and operation. For example, Munich Re has been a very active investor in different types of insurtechs and has provided reinsurance capacity for many of the tech-enabled new carriers like Lemonade and Root.

The acquisition of startups by incumbents will extend beyond carriers, with innovative intermediaries being attractive acquisitions for traditional brokers and agents, like Marsh buying Dovetail in 2015 and Aon buying CoverWallet in 2019.

Finally, this pattern is likely to extend to insurtechs that provide enabling innovations that get acquired by larger tech companies, like Guidewire buying Cyence, FirstBest and EagleEye. It is feasible to see a player like Salesforce, who is very active in the Insurance vertical and has a large presence at ITC, being an acquirer of sales- and service-enabling insurtechs, for example.

Not all startups (including startup carriers) will be acquired by incumbents, of course. However, I do think we are less likely to see today's startup carriers a decade from now as independent, established carriers. Instead, incumbents with the financial wherewithal to make nine-figure-or-larger purchases will see acquisition of innovators as a way to speed up their evolution.

Some of these acquisitions will be successful in driving change in the acquiring company. However, buying an innovator does not make you innovative. Quite often, the innovative spirit and drive of the acquired company is snuffed out by the acquirer's lack of cultural flexibility and openness. That is true of acquisitions in any industry, not just our own.

It is precisely those two things, flexibility and openness, that are required to be willing to follow the advice gleaned from the cases in this book around listening to your customers, engaging with your people and staying focused on intention, outcome and time.

Whether you evolve organically or use acquisition to jump forward in a single transaction, without embracing these innovative principles, your evolutionary momentum will fizzle out.

Ultimately, we will see some new players who are here for the long-haul, and some who are not (whether that is because they do not make it or because they get acquired). From both those who do and do not make it, we will learn about new approaches, ideas and solutions, and the industry will move forward.

We will also see incumbent players who continue to be here for the long-haul, and some who will not (whether that is because they do not make it or are acquired by a someone who does).

One thing will be consistent across both startups and incumbents who are successful down the line. They will have evolved individually *and* helped the overall industry evolve. Seeking ways to evolve your organization through working with your customers, engaging your people and staying focused on delivering meaningful change is the best path to being part of the future of insurance.

ACKNOWLEDGMENTS

I'd like to acknowledge several people who helped inspire and push me to write this book, and others who contributed directly and indirectly to it. First, the entire team at The Insurance Nerds who listened to me talk about an idea about how to help insurers evolve and immediately wanted to support my work. My friend Nick Lamparelli, who was part of the Insurance Nerds (who were the original publishers of this book) at the time barely let me finish explaining the idea before saying yes, and Carly Burham and Tony Cañas jumped in with their support as soon as I shared the idea with them. Carly was then there throughout the journey, providing guidance, support, structure and an incredibly-valuable sounding board (including fielding my many long-winded Slack messages as I thought though things).

Kevin Kerridge of Hiscox, who has always inspired me with his mind, his values and his approach to leadership, did not bat an eye when I reached out about sharing some thoughts for the book, and went over and above by helping me refine the concept and think about potential stories to enrich the context-setting section of the book. I am lucky to have gotten to work alongside Kevin, and am continuing that lucky streak with his consistent support whenever I reach out.

Andy Pinkes, who has given of himself as a mentor and guide throughout the years not only helped with developing ideas in the book during its early stages, but immediately offered to make a number of connections that directly impacted the final product, including introducing me to Jérémy Jawish of Shift. I'm fairly certain I have yet to return a single favor Andy has done for me, yet he continues to be gracious with his help and guidance repeatedly. I did do him one favor by not referring to him in this book as "industry legend, Andy Pinkes," but I suppose I just called him that indirectly, so I will continue to be in his debt.

Anne Blume, CEO of the CLM, has been an unwavering support to me since literally the day we met at the CLM CCO Summit back in 2018. Anne has been someone I could think through ideas with, and get honest feedback that directly helped me on my mission. When I first told her about this project, she was supportive and gave me several thoughts about who to talk to and what to think about as I dove into this project.

Jeff Goldberg of Novarica is someone I got to meet during a core system project at a prior carrier, and assumed I would not have much chance to interact with again. While I was at Hi Marley, Jeff and Stephanie Dalwin at Novarica spent a lot of time sharing ideas with me, hearing about what we were working on at Hi Marley, and both of them gave so much of their time and insight to put into this book before it even had a name.

Before I name the people and companies who shared honestly and openly in the cases in this book, there are some people whose contributions were as-important despite not being mentioned in the cases. John Emery, who has been an innovator in the insurance space, introduced me to stories of innovation and innovative people in the industry I was not aware of that directly lead to some of the cases you read in this book.

Basilios Manousogiannakis saw the idea of the book, and being part of Chris Champlin's team, knew what EMPLOYERS was working on would fit what I was hoping to share. He spent time with me (including getting to meet in person in Boston, which was great), but also stewarded the idea through EMPLOYERS, helping get people on board with the idea and making sure Ray and Chris were primed to share the kind of real insights that differentiate a case based on first-hand knowledge from one written through literature searches and reinterpreting press releases.

Tanguy Catlin, Senior Partner in McKinsey & Company's insurance practice and someone I'm proud to call a friend since we worked together way back in the mid-2000s, was amazingly giving, thoughtful and helpful. Despite having just gotten home from a marathon set of trips and transcontinental flights, he spent time to share thoughts about the innovation going on globally, what dynamics were at play, what could differentiate those who succeed and those who struggle, and then went on to introduce me to Caribou Honig, who has been incredibly helpful and giving of his time, which is already in high demand.

Another crucial supporter is Steven Hunckler at the State Compensation Insurance Fund of California. Steve and I met a few years ago at the CLM's CCO Summit, and stayed connected since then. Steve has always been responsive to my outreach, took time from his day to have breakfast with me when I happened to be out his way, and immediately volunteered to help bring a case study on innovation at SCIF into the book. After giving of himself to talk about a game-changing initiative his Claims team is bringing to market called URConnected, Steve set aside his own story and connected me with SCIF CEO Vern Steiner to learn about SCIF's journey with Quote and Bind in their Direct business. Steve has continued to be supportive, helping to steward the case to completion.

And while I'm on the topic of SCIF, although he is named in the case, I'd be remiss not to thank Vern personally, too. He and I spoke years ago on another project, and he was equally excited, visionary and supportive. Despite everything on his plate, including dealing with the COVID-19 pandemic, which became an issue impacting SCIF in many ways, Vern has always responded to me quickly, meaningfully and helpfully. Dante Robinson and Cameron Anthony, who are featured in the SCIF case, as well, were equally giving, thoughtful and responsive.

The same has to be said of the team at Ohio Mutual. While I am speaking specifically about those I worked with on developing this case – CEO Mark Russell, VP of Claims John DeLucia and his team members, Andrea Presler, Kate Dodson and Kim Dallas – I actually mean this about OMIG more broadly. Having been in their offices a few times and having gotten to work directly with many members of the Ohio Mutual team, I can say that the entire company is worthy of thanks for what they have given me throughout my relationship with them.

When John Emery opened a relationship for me with Brian Gaab at CSAA, I did not know that I was connecting with the person who would end up sharing the first case I would write for this book. Brian gave hours of his time despite so many things on his plate, and helped see the case through the approval process at CSAA quickly and smoothly (and thanks to Jason Willett for making the CSAA review as easy and helpful as it was).

Andy Pinkes was not still at CNA when I started work on that case, but he had introduced me to Rob Thomas while he still was. I knew I would be dealing with someone great if Andy had hired them, and Rob was exactly that. Rob dedicated the time it took to share what was a very detailed story of their journey with Shift, but also worked internally with their Communication and Legal teams to make sure the final case was as good as it is, and did so in record time.

The same is true of Gary Kaplan, Justin Gress and Rose Hall at AXA XL. All three of them spent time with me to give me more than just the details of the case, but the broader context and intention that the case fit into. Gary has also taken time with me to give me more understanding and insight about the RRI approach, which has helped me see how this tool was so pivotal to their continued ability to innovate at AXA XL Construction.

Andy Pinkes gets another thanks for introducing me to Andy Cohen, COO at Snapsheet. Andy gave me far too much of his time on what was a really interesting conversation about the state of innovation in the industry and where things are headed. He also graciously and selflessly introduced me to Luke Harris at USAA.

Luke was such a great help in sharing a story of how USAA approaches innovation he is clearly proud of, but also for going out of his way to share valuable background articles with me, and for helping me navigate through other great people at the company like Lara Hendrickson and CCO Sean Burgess for the approval needed to participate in a project like this. I got a very clear sense from everyone I have interacted with at USAA that their dedication to and the empowerment they feel from their mission is not just talk. It literally drives everything they do.

I would also like to thank the people at carriers not seen in this book who gave of their time to share their stories, but ultimately were not able to because of internal considerations around what they do and do not share publicly. I obviously cannot name them, but I know they know who they are, and they have been fantastic to work with and supported this project in other ways.

The same goes for many people I spoke with in researching the ideas of the book whose names do not ultimately appear in the text despite providing invaluable insight.

As with everything I take on professionally, I need to recognize and thank my family for supporting me and understanding when I would disappear into the basement to write for hours at a time. Or, worse yet, when I would emerge eager to talk about all the cool insurance things I was working on. They indulged me repeatedly despite not really being interested personally in what I was excited about. My poor wife heard more insurance stuff than any non-insurance person should have to be subjected to, and she took it all like a champ!

I have to thank all of the amazing people at the many insurance carriers and insurtech solution providers featured here and beyond who work tirelessly to help people in need. The work can be hard, it can be thankless, and it is not easy, but we do it every day. Thanks to those efforts, families have a home to sleep in again, people have transportation they depend on working again so they can go about their lives, companies can serve their market without fear of being put out of business because of a property loss or lawsuit, injured workers can get the care they need to get back to work – and their life – again. And we do all of it despite the barriers we face, despite jokes about the industry not being cool or exciting, and despite the threat of new technology or competitors being predicted to put us out of work. It is hard, yet very important work the people of the insurance ecosystem do every day for those who depend on us to keep doing it.

And, lastly, I want to thank you, the readers, for taking in my thoughts and hopefully thinking about how you can bring them into your context to spark evolution in your situation. It is through the work of individual people and your dedication to making things better that we will ensure the future of insurance is what our customers expect and want it to be while remaining an enriching and valuable space to build a career with a purpose.

ABOUT THE AUTHOR

Bryan Falchuk is a best-selling author, speaker and consultant to the Insurance industry on the subject of innovation as the founder and Managing Partner of Insurance Evolution Partners. He has written for many top publications like Inc. Magazine, The Chicago Tribune, LA Times and more, been a guest on over 200 podcasts and radio shows, hosts his own show, and has presented multiple TEDx  Talks. His first two books, the best-selling *Do a Day* and *The 50 75 100 Solution: Build Better Relationships*, have won numerous awards and, more importantly, continue to help people change their lives for the better, every day.

Bryan spent 20 years in the insurance industry where he was most recently Head of Claims for Hiscox USA before joining AI-enabled insurtech communications provider Hi Marley to help drive their growth. With his unique experience at both carriers and insurtechs, he brings his perspective to bear to help the industry evolve in a market that facing disruption and change. Prior to Hiscox, Bryan held leadership roles in corporate strategy, operations and distribution at Liberty Mutual, Beazley and Coverys, and served as a management consultant to several top carriers as part of McKinsey & Company's insurance practice. Bryan is also an advisor and board member of several technology startups serving the insurance industry.

Bryan holds an MBA from the Tuck School of Business at Dartmouth College and a BA in Economics from Bowdoin College. Learn more about Bryan at bryanfalchuk.com, and follow him on social media at @bryanfalchuk.

Subscribe to The Future of Insurance Podcast
future-of-insurance.com/podcast

Get Updates on Future Volumes in The FOI Series:
future-of-insurance.com/updates

Connect with Bryan Falchuk
Web: bryanfalchuk.com
Facebook: facebook.com/bryanfalchuk
LinkedIn: linkedin.com/in/bryanfalchuk
Instagram: instagram.com/bryanfalchuk
Twitter: twitter.com/bryanfalchuk

Also by Bryan Falchuk
Do a Day: How to Live a Better Life Every Day
The 50 75 100 Solution: Build Better Relationships

Connect with Insurance Evolution Partners
Web: insurance-evolution.com
Facebook: facebook.com/insureevolve
LinkedIn: linkedin.com/company/insureevolve
Instagram: instagram.com/insureevolve
Twitter: twitter.com/insureevolve

Made in the USA
Columbia, SC
16 November 2022

71440421R00095